PUB

The W,
and Forest of Dean

Paul Traynor

COUNTRYSIDE BOOKS

NEWBURY, BERKSHIRE

First published 1996
©Paul Traynor 1996

COUNTRYSIDE BOOKS
3 Catherine Road
Newbury, Berkshire

ISBN 1 85306 411 4

Designed by Mon Mohan
Cover illustration by Colin Doggett
Photographs and maps by the author

Produced through MRM Associates Ltd., Reading
Typeset by Paragon Typesetters, Newton-le-Willows, Merseyside
Printed by J. W. Arrowsmith, Bristol

Contents

Introduction

Walk 1   Pwllmeyric: The New Inn (3 miles)   8

    2   Chepstow: The Three Tuns Inn (4½ miles)   13

    3   Brockweir: The Brockweir Country Inn (2 miles)   18

    4   Llandogo: The Sloop Inn (2½ miles)   23

    5   St Briavels: The George (2½ miles)   27

    6   The Narth: The Trekkers Inn (2 miles)   32

    7   Clearwell: The Wyndham Arms (2½ miles)   36

    8   Parkend: The Woodman (4 miles)   40

    9   Moseley Green: The Rising Sun (2½ miles)   45

    10   Newland: The Ostrich (3½ miles)   50

    11   Upper Soudley: The White Horse Inn (2 miles)   54

    12   The Speech House Hotel (3 miles)   58

    13   Staunton: The White Horse (2½ miles)   62

    14   Symond's Yat: The Saracen's Head (2 miles)   66

15	Goodrich: Ye Hostelrie (2½ miles)	71
16	Howle Hill: The Crown (2½ miles)	75
17	Ross-on-Wye: The Hope and Anchor (2 miles)	79
18	Carey: The Cottage of Content (3 miles)	83
19	Fownhope: The Green Man (3 miles)	87
20	Mordiford: The Moon Inn (4 miles)	91

Publisher's Note

We hope that you obtain considerable enjoyment from this book; great care has been taken in its preparation. However, changes of landlord and actual closures are sadly not uncommon. Likewise, although at the time of publication all routes followed public rights of way or permitted paths, diversion orders can be made and permissions withdrawn.

We cannot of course be held responsible for such diversion orders and any inaccuracies in the text which result from these or any other changes to the routes nor any damage which might result from walkers trespassing on private property. We are anxious though that all details covering the walks and the pubs are kept up to date and would therefore welcome information from readers which would be relevant to future editions.

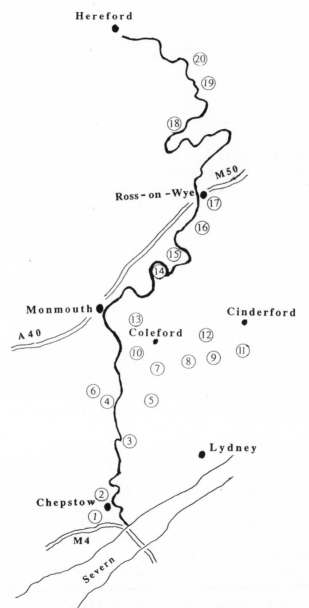

Area map showing the locations of the walks.

Introduction

The Wye Valley and Forest of Dean – we are fortunate indeed that Nature has left us these two areas of enchanting beauty to explore and enjoy in such close proximity. And what better way to do it than on foot, with a drink and a bite to eat as an added incentive.

The Wye – fast-flowing through deep gorges in the south, broad and slow-moving as it meanders through pastures further north – has bewitched visitors for centuries. The romantic poets fell in love with it, and so have many generations ever since. In the selection of walks, I have tried to offer glimpses of the Wye Valley in all its guises. In turn they visit high vantage points and riverside meadows, historic sites such as Tintern Abbey and tiny, picturesque hamlets. There is, of course, much more to the Wye Valley than any one book can convey – I hope readers, with appetite whetted, will want to explore further.

The Forest of Dean, too, is an area of many parts and its differing roles over the years have bequeathed a fascinating legacy. Beneath the vast canopy of green are the marks of its past – a cradle of industry, royal hunting forest, timber supplier for shipping and the coalfields. A maze of trails for walkers and riders awaits today's visitors who, like me, are likely to be amazed to learn that the last major coal mine closed as recently as 1965! The walks described here touch on all that 'heritage'.

All the walks are short and should present no difficulties for anyone in average physical shape. It's wise to wear sensible footwear – walking boots or wellingtons – and carrying a waterproof jacket is recommended.

The route descriptions are thorough and should safely lead you around each circuit. The sketch maps are intended as a rough guide only and should be used in conjunction with the relevant OS map, which will, in any case, be handy for tracking down pubs in areas beyond the scope of road atlases.

Pub opening hours are not given because, these days, they are liable to frequent change. Some pubs open all day at weekends but not midweek, others have different regimes according to season – and can even vary due to inclement weather! If you're making a long journey to a pub, it's worth a call in advance to check on times, especially if you'd like to eat outside normal hours – 12 noon to 2 pm and 7 pm to 9 pm.

While walkers are always welcome, muddy boots may be less warmly received; a swift changeover at the car boot only takes a moment. Similarly landlords are usually happy for their car parks to be used as walking bases, but most appreciate a quiet word in advance – and all, quite understandably, expect your custom at some stage!

Walking, eating and drinking are some of life's greatest pleasures. I hope all three bring you as much enjoyment as I have had in preparing this book.

Paul Traynor
Spring 1996

1 Pwllmeyric
The New Inn

This friendly village local has an unusual claim to fame – probably the plushest, most luxurious seating you're likely to come across in a pub. The grand easy chairs in the lounge make first-class aeroplane seats look like humble bar stools, and there's a reason. The chairs come from an ocean liner, the Canadian Pacific *Empress of France* which was broken up in 1962.

And it's not just the chairs which catch the eye – there's fine wood panelling on the walls, various fittings and even port and starboard lights above the bar. Sipping a drink in the high-ceilinged lounge, you half expect an invitation to a game of shuffle-board or cocktails with the captain! Fortunately there's nothing snobby about the New Inn and you don't have to dress for dinner!

In contrast to the lounge, the bar, with a low, beamed ceiling, exposed stone walls and wooden settles has a lived-in feel. It's actually the original pub, dating back to when it earned its keep as a coaching inn. The pub has been much extended and now takes in what was once a separate smithy.

Food is plentiful and good value. There are separate lunch and evening menus, though this is not stuck to rigidly. At lunch you can choose from enormous doorstep sandwiches or pub standards like deep fried plaice or Cumberland sausage and mash, with vegetarian options such as cauliflower cheese or tagliatelle in tomato, herb and cream sauce. In the evening some Welsh options stand out from steaks and the like – try for instance Brythyll Wedi Ei Rwymo Mewn Bacun (fresh Welsh trout wrapped in streaky bacon). Specials available at lunchtime and in the evening might include chicken en croûte, ocean pie or steak and ale pie. Children may have half portions or choose fish fingers, burgers and so on.

This Ushers house serves Ushers' Best and Founders bitters, with a seasonal special from the brewery and there's also Guinness, Kronenbourg 1664 and Strongbow cider.

Telephone: 01291 622670.

How to get there: The New Inn really cannot be missed beside the A48 on the western fringe of the the village of Pwllmeyric, about 2 miles south-west of the centre of Chepstow.

Parking: The pub has a large car park at the rear.

Length of the walk: 3 miles. Map: OS Landranger 162 Gloucester and Forest of Dean; OS Pathfinder 1131 Chepstow (inn GR 515922).

The pretty little valley of Mounton Brook makes a lovely start for this walk – and a startling contrast to the busy A48 left behind. An easy walk which takes in a variety of rural scenery in this quiet corner of Gwent.

The Walk

With your back to the front of the pub cross the A48 carefully and turn right along the pavement towards Chepstow. After about 300 yards look out on the left for a public footpath signpost, set back a little off the road, indicating 'Mounton church 0.8 km'. Cross the stile and bear right, walking up the attractive vale with Mounton Brook on your left and a wooded bank on your right.

Walk on down the well-walked path, ignoring a stile in the fence on the right (that's used on the return leg), trending rightwards away from the brook towards the right-hand corner of the field.

9

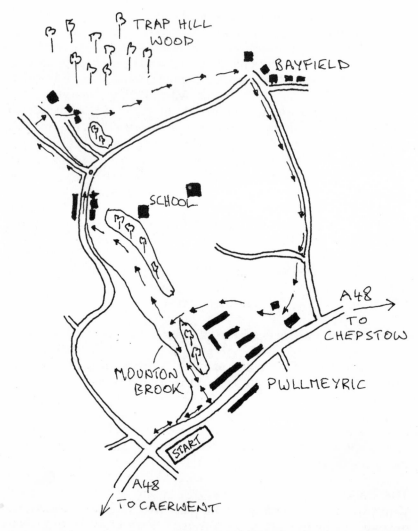

Cross a stile and continue with fencing on the right, soon veering left to pass to the left of a cottage. Cross a stile and concrete footbridge over the brook beside the cottage to reach a metalled lane and turn right.

Pass Mounton church and a series of attractive cottages to reach a mini-roundabout – which looks a little out of place in this quiet setting. The name Mounton is apparently derived from Monkstown

Mounton Brook.

– from the time when the land belonged to the priory of Chepstow. Take the left turn at the roundabout signposted to Shirenewton. After a couple of minutes walking up this gently rising lane, look on the right for a public footpath signpost and hop over the stile into a paddock. There's a sequence of stiles here which sounds complex but is clearly waymarked and easy to follow on the ground.

Cross the paddock to a rustic stile and continue down the field to a footbridge over the brook. Walk straight on, over another stile, to a path on the left edge of a garden. After a few yards up the garden path you reach a path junction with stiles to left and right. Take the right-hand option, go through a scrappy patch of land with outbuildings and carry on up the path which climbs quite steeply through a profusion of holly. You soon clamber to the top of this rise and cross a stile to enter a broad field. Continue with the hedge on the left, enjoying the open views across pastures and woods.

Cross a stile in the left corner of the field and continue across the next field, aiming slightly right for a cluster of houses and farms ahead which is the hamlet of Bayfield. Cross a stile beside a gate and bear right – do not take the lane immediately on the right, but walk on up past the houses to reach a small junction of minor roads near Broadhurst cottage with a tiny triangular patch of grass forming another mini-roundabout. Turn right here onto a very narrow lane.

After about half a mile or so along the hedge-lined lane pass on your right the gateway to Brynderwen Bigwood and shortly beyond it cross a stile on the right to reach a metalled drive. Bear obliquely left up and across the drive to reach on the right an unusual metal squeeze stile set in iron railings.

Hop through and in the field beyond trend left to a stile by a gate between houses. Walk on down a patch of grass, cross directly over a rough access drive and continue ahead, with garden fence panelling and then a line of conifers on your left to reach and cross another stile into a field.

Continue down the slope, with a newish housing estate on the left, to another stile in the bottom left corner and then veer left past a water trough along the top of a pronounced bank. Shortly after passing a shallow bowl depression on the right, bear obliquely right to descend the bank and reach a line of fencing. Turn left here along the bottom of the bank to soon reach a stile – the one passed on the outward leg. Cross over and turn left towards the village along the path used earlier but with the brook now on your right. Back at the A48 turn right, crossing carefully at some stage, to return to the New Inn.

Chepstow
The Three Tuns Inn

There's nothing false or fancy about this cheery pub, close to the river and within an arrowshot of Chepstow Castle. Its position, and beer garden with children's play area at the back, means it attracts a good number of visitors. But the Three Tuns, like any good town pub, also has its regulars and can be quite lively.

Simply furnished with wooden tables and chairs, the open-plan bar naturally divides into the drinking end by the bar itself, and an eating section with plenty of tables. A poolroom at the back completes this quite small pub's facilities.

On the food side good value is a priority. If walking gives you a hearty appetite, why not consider the 20 oz mixed grill – pork and lamb chops, gammon, steak, liver, sausage, egg, mushrooms, tomatoes, and chips or boiled potatoes – but you may have to do the walk twice to work off that lot! The very reasonably priced four-course Sunday roast lunch also takes some eating. Other options include Gwent hot pot (like the Lancashire favourite with a local twist), steak, kidney and ale pie, liver and bacon grill, and curries like chicken tikka masala or lamb masala. Specials chalked up daily may include the likes of pork fillet in cider sauce and venison in red wine or port sauce. Vegetarians might choose from mushroom stroganoff, nutloaf or vegetable lasagne.

Children may have half portions of these main meals, or opt for sausage and chips, egg and chips and other favourites. A point to note is that food is not available on Friday and Saturday evenings.

Bass is the regular real ale at this Greenalls house, with occasional guests such as Smiles Best Bitter. Bulmer's Traditional and Strongbow ciders, Murphy's stout, Flowers Best Bitter and Stella Artois and Heineken lagers are also served.

Telephone: 01291 623497.

How to get there: Chepstow lies at the mouth of the river Wye and is easily accessible from the A466, A48 or M4. The town has a one-way system and the easiest way to find the pub is to follow signs to the castle – the pub cannot be missed to the left of the castle car park entrance.

Parking: The pub is located beside a large public car park (free).

Length of the walk: About 4½ miles. Map: OS Landranger 162 Gloucester and Forest of Dean (inn GR 536942).

A delightful walk visiting the Lancaut Peninsula, one of the most beautiful and tranquil stretches of the Wye. The circuit also takes in a nature reserve and sections of the Offa's Dyke National Trail. A visit to splendid Chepstow Castle is highly recommended.

The Walk

From the front of the pub, walk left down the main road towards the river. Cross the broad Wye by the attractive metal-railed bridge ahead of you, pausing for a great view of Chepstow Castle – a good spot for a photo. At the far end of the bridge, cross the road and take a narrow lane opposite, climbing steadily between walls. Part of the way up the lane you join the Offa's Dyke path coming in from the right. Continue up the lane and soon reach the A48. Cross directly over and carry on up a country lane, waymarked ODP. As you approach some houses cross a stile on the left into a field, and then bear right up the slope with homes and trees on your right.

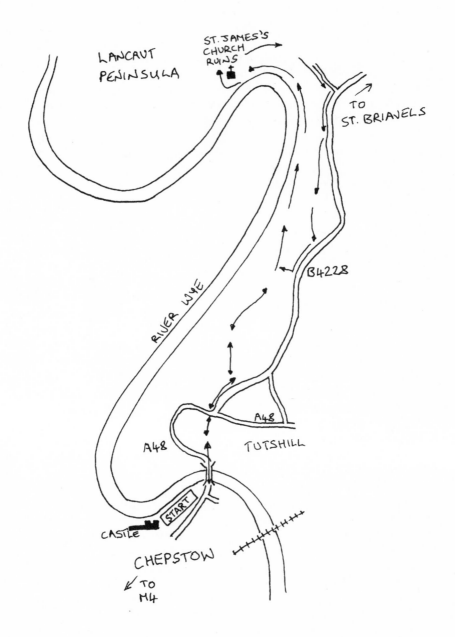

LANCAUT
PENINSULA

ST. JAMES'S
CHURCH
RUINS

TO
ST. BRIAVELS

B4228

RIVER WYE

A48

A48

TUTSHILL

START

CASTLE

CHEPSTOW

TO
M4

Ruined Tutshill Tower comes into view on the right (fenced off), which was probably at one time a watch-tower for the castle on the other side of the river.

The path soon becomes clearer, heading towards the left-hand corner of the field. Cross a stile shaded by trees to the right of a stone wall, then continue with the wall on your left. At the end of the wall, cross a stile on the left to enter a narrow passage between a fence and wall. After a few yards the waymarked path turns right, follows a short stretch of surfaced drive, then crosses a stile on the left to enter another field. This well walked path traverses the pasture with a fine house – Pen Moel – drawing the eye to the right. At the top left-hand corner of the field cross a stile to join a narrow path. The Offa's Dyke path bears right and the walk later returns to this point. However, turn left here, passing under a rustic wooden footbridge to enter Lancaut Nature Reserve.

The clear path starts a long descent through very attractive deciduous woodland, offering glimpses of the river through the trees to the left and passing below impressive cliffs and quarry walls to the right. Stay on the main path, eventually reaching the riverside and continue along its bank. A small, jumbled rockfall requires some agility to cross – yellow painted waymarks aid your progress. Carry on as the path rises and falls tracking the river on the left. There are a number of little paths around here, either heading right to cliffs used by rock climbers, or left to the river edge. Ignore these and remain on the main path which is easy to follow. The path swings left following a broad loop in the river and this section was alive with squirrels when we last walked it. Pass a few grassy riverside banks, or use them as an excuse for a break to admire the view across the broad, slow-moving river, eventually reaching an unusual metal stile built by an army unit.

Shortly beyond the stile turn right away from the river – a yellow arrow on an old post indicates the way – to reach the ruins of St James's church. An explanatory table beside a stone stile in the churchyard wall tells the story of this atmospheric spot. The church fell into disuse in the mid-19th century (hardly surprising considering the distinct absence of nearby parishioners!), but its history could well go way back. The building has been dated back to the late 12th century but the site has been associated with a 6th-century Welsh holy man – St Cewydd. It's certainly a place for quiet contemplation even now.

Walk on up to the left of the churchyard and then swing right to pass above it. Beyond a bench, dedicated to the memory of voluntary warden Les Darbourn, the path rises diagonally right to enter woodland via another metal stile. The clear path climbs steadily through the trees to a T-junction with a level path. Turn right, passing old kilns on your left, and continue climbing to a country lane where you turn right.

You soon pass some houses, with those on the right enjoying some of the most spectacular views in the country. Control envy and walk on with views opening up ahead across the Bristol Channel. Soon reach the B4228 where you turn right, signposted to Chepstow. This is a busy little road requiring care but you soon leave it, taking a narrow path on the right signposted to Sedbury Cliffs – you are now back on the Offa's Dyke Path.

As the path leaves the road and goes left round the back of house, a path heads a short way to the right to Wintour's Leap, a rocky promontory overlooking the Wye with panoramic views. The story has it that this was the spot where, during the English Civil War, local Royalist Sir John Wintour evaded capture by jumping on horseback and swimming the river a long way below. Unless Sir John was also an unsung early exponent of equestrian hang-gliding the story seems wholly unlikely. Keep a close eye on children here as a repeat performance is not recommended. The path continues behind homes and gardens, passes through a metal kissing-gate, and then proceeds along the thoroughly fenced-off rim of sheer quarry workings. On reaching a drive with a house on the right, go straight on down a green lane, almost entirely enclosed with arching holly and vegetation.

Go through two kissing-gates and soon emerge, via a gate and a little archway, onto the B4228 again. Turn right and walk down beside the road for a short while. Keep an eye out on the right for the entrance to Pen Moel, the grand house passed on the outward leg. Beside it, take the path (signposted Offa's Dyke Path) between railings and a wall. This path soon brings you back to the stile by the rustic footbridge passed earlier. Go left over the stile to retrace steps to Chepstow.

The return route is clearly signposted Offa's Dyke Path, until it leaves the steep lane descending to the river bridge. Carry straight on down to cross the bridge and keep ahead to the pub and car park.

Brockweir
The Brockweir Country Inn

It is hard to believe that the quiet, scattered village of Brockweir was at one time a bustling port and boat-building centre – even a den of iniquity – but that's the case. Before road and rail the river was a vital means of transport. The Wye is still tidal at Brockweir and sailing barges and boats used the village quay to transfer cargo to flat-bottomed barges which were then, incredibly, towed by men as far as Hereford and even Hay on Wye.

Thirsty work, one imagines, and the village is believed to have had a good number of cider houses and a lurid reputation. So much so that a church (near the pub) was founded by the Protestant Bristol Moravians in 1831 with a mission to sort out the 'ungodly' inhabitants! They seem a pretty respectable bunch these days and the Brockweir Country Inn, just 20 yards from the river, has a quiet, laid-back atmosphere, ideal to enjoy a relaxing drink and bite to eat.

The pub building is some 400 years old, but the inn doesn't make a meal of the village's history. The small bar with pool table is simply furnished and has one of a number of old church pews dotted around the place. The lounge is much larger, traditionally decorated, with no fake trimmings – some of the great beams are from a sailing barge and even the guns on the wall are real. It is also carpeted so muddy boots are best left outside. The flagged beer garden and covered courtyard at the rear are popular with walkers, and large groups are welcome to book a comfortable room upstairs.

Walkers form an important part of the pub's custom – the Offa's Dyke Path passes by – and the menu emphasis is on freshly cooked food which can be prepared and delivered quickly. Starters might feature pâté and toast or tomato soup, whereas main meals could include local beef cooked in stout or lamb balti. Non-meat eaters have options such as tuna bake and salad and plaice and chips to choose from. Regular real ales are Freeminer and Hook Norton Best, which accompany guest beers such as Greene King Abbot Ale or Morland Old Speckled Hen. There's also Bulmer's Traditional Cider, Iron Oak cider, Grolsch lager, Guinness and various keg beers. The inn offers accommodation in two doubles and one single room.

Telephone: 01291 689548.

How to get there: Brockweir village lies on the east bank of the river Wye, north of Tintern and is connected by bridge to the A466 Monmouth-Chepstow road on the far bank. It is also accessible by road from the east via the B4228 south of St Briavels. The pub can be found near the bridge.

Parking: The pub has a small car park (a mention to the landlord if you're leaving the car there while walking is preferred) and there is some roadside parking space nearby. If you have difficulty there is a layby off the A466 on the other side and just north of the bridge.

Length of the walk: 2 miles. Map: OS Landranger 162 Gloucester and Forest of Dean (inn GR 541012).

This fascinating walk takes you alongside the river, passing old Tintern railway station, to the celebrated abbey ruins. The return route follows an ancient woodland track – the Monk's Way – linking the abbey with Brockweir village where the monks had a farm.

The old railway station at Tintern.

The Walk

With your back to the pub entrance, turn left and cross the bridge. Immediately beyond it, cross an unusual wooden, yoke-shaped stile on the left and descend steps. A path to the left follows the river bank to Tintern, but you continue straight ahead along the line of the old railway, following a broad well surfaced track. Soon reach a good play area with swings and climbing frames, then the old Tintern station signal box comes into view, looking just like a train set accessory. Opposite the box is the old station building, now offering refreshments, and just beyond are some old carriages and wagons, now housing various displays, information and crafts – well worth a few minutes' exploration.

Proceed in the same direction, with a mini-railway track on your left, until you approach what looks like the end of the line – a bench with a fence behind. In fact, the path drops down steps on your right towards the river bank. Go through a gate and immediately cross a stile on the right. Walk on with the river on the left and fenced-off pasture on the right. The path uses three little bridges to cross streams and as you approach a church, climb a stile and continue with the church on your right, leaving the churchyard

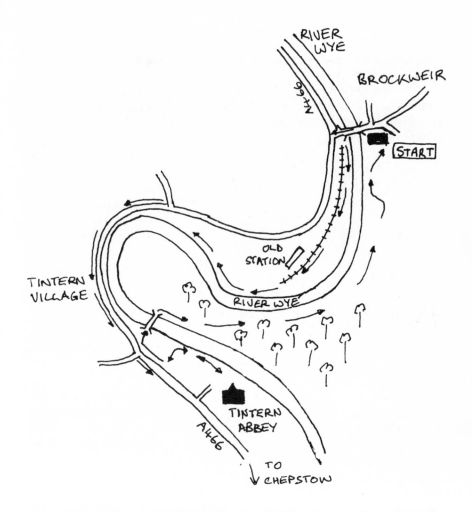

by a gate. Proceed straight ahead and follow waymarkers through lanes to emerge on the main road.

Turn left and follow the road through attractive Tintern village, pausing to browse in the bookshops and galleries on the way. By crossing the road a couple of times it is possible to stay on pavement almost the whole way through the village – in summer the road can be quite busy. Shortly after passing a bridge (you cross this later) and Abbey Mill turn left. Pass the Riverside Centre and go more or less straight on down a path heading towards the river. This path soon swings right in front of cottages and emerges at a roundabout with a cider press in its centre. In front of you is the

Tintern Abbey entrance and shop with the evocative ruins to the right – a visit is recommended.

From the abbey complex entrance retrace your steps along the Tintern Trail to the main road. Turn right and after a short distance, just beyond the Abbey Mill, turn right (not the immediate right which drops down to the mill), to join a path leading to the white-painted bridge. (Incidentally, monks would have used a ferry crossing which operated near the Anchor Inn). Cross over and follow the path ahead, soon to reach a crossing of paths. Ignore the left and immediate right paths and take the other right-hand path, waymarked to Devil's Pulpit.

This broad track runs parallel to the river, which is located a fair distance away on your right. Before you get level with the abbey ruins across the river, look out on the left for metal posts and a side path, signposted Devil's Pulpit. Follow this rocky track, climbing into the woods. The path climbs for a while then swings right, giving views of the river Wye below to the left – the meandering Wye can be quite surprising! You will soon come to a Y-junction of paths beside a stone parapet, where you take the left option to join a broad, well surfaced track. After several minutes on this track, with a wooded hillside on your right, the path starts to descend. Go through a gate and shortly afterwards cross a stile on your left. Walk directly ahead down a sloping field to the river and turn right along a path on the bank. As you approach Brockweir village, cross a stile next to a line of conifers and keep to the path, which weaves between fences past the Moravian church to emerge onto a road. Bear left to reach the pub.

4 Llandogo
The Sloop Inn

As its name suggests this popular pub once relied for trade, not on the adjacent road, but instead looked the other way to traffic on the river it overlooks. Llandogo, now a tranquil village of pretty homes largely scattered on the hillside, was once a busy port. The Sloop, which dates back at least to the 18th century, recalls the shallow-bottomed vessels which shuttled mostly between the Wye settlements and Bristol.

The pub is quite a large place, with a simple front bar and a more comfortable lounge at the rear, which is largely used by diners. The modern furnishings are unlikely to set the pulse racing but the view from panoramic windows over the good beer garden to the river Wye is lovely, so arrive early for a sought after window seat.

Food is wholesome and local produce is used when possible, so if salmon is on the specials board it may have been caught by the landlord, an enthusiastic fisherman. Fish is regularly available, including locally farmed rainbow trout fried in butter, fillet of breaded sole filled with crab meat and seafood sauce and fillet of breaded plaice filled with prawn and mushroom sauce. Alongside pub standards like steaks, grills, lasagne and chilli, you will find chicken balti with naan bread, local prime cooked ham and pasta carbonara with ham and mushrooms in a cream sauce. For vegetarians the choice includes vegetable moussaka, pasta bake and mushroom balti. There is no children's menu as such, but things like fish fingers are usually available, or meals may be split for children to share with spare plates provided.

This award-winning freehouse has a reputation for good beer. Regular beers are Bass and Wye Valley Bitter, plus a guest brew, such as Fuller's London Pride or Mansfield Old Baily. Also at the bar are Guinness, draught Bulmer's Original cider and Dortmunder Union lager. The inn offers accommodation in four en suite bedrooms, including one with a four-poster bed.

Telephone: 01594 530291.

How to get there: The inn is situated beside the A466 in the village of Llandogo, halfway between Monmouth and Chepstow.

Parking: The Sloop has a large car park opposite.

Length of the walk: 2½ miles. Map: OS Landranger 162 Gloucester and Forest of Dean (inn GR 526041).

A lot of variety on this circuit which includes fine woodland views, pretty Cleddon Falls and a beautiful zigzag descent of a wooded gorge. Note: The level of the water in the little stream beside the Sloop is a good indicator of whether the falls above are in spate or not.

The Walk
With your back to the front of the pub, cross the road and take the small lane to the right of the car park. The lane passes the remains of a cider press and emerges, after a couple of minutes, onto a road. Go left and continue along the road past a signpost on the right to Cleddon Shoots Reserve. You will emerge at that point towards the end of the walk. The road climbs gently, with fine views to the left over the village and the river Wye, and you will soon pass beneath majestic conifers. The road bears to the right, passing a signpost for

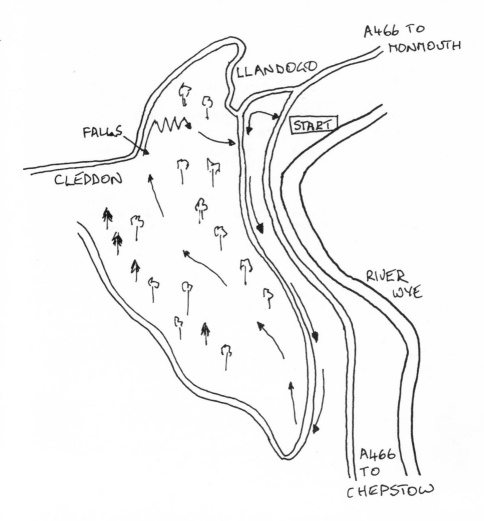

the Wye Valley Walk, and you soon reach the entrance to the Forestry Commission's Whitestones parking area on your right. Head right through the lower parking area, with a toilet block on the left, and follow the forest road as it swings right climbing through the trees. You soon approach the main parking area on your right which has an excellent adventure play area, information display and picnic benches.

Bear left away from the car park to go through a gate beside a barrier and follow the clear track ahead. This passes a series of viewpoints to the right, the third and last being the most impressive,

25

affording great views across treetops and the river. Shortly beyond that viewpoint turn right onto a clear path, waymarked Wye Valley Walk. The path soon enters woods, continuing between low stone walls, passing houses on the left and right to reach the little hamlet of Cleddon. Cross the stream which forms the cascades and gorge you soon descend beside, then immediately turn right down wooden steps and bear left to pass under an amazing old beech tree, which has grown above and around huge blocks of stone – quite a sight.

The path climbs a short hop to reach a broad track where you turn right. You are now following a clear, well graded track – probably a mule or donkey track at one time – which zigzags down the hillside through very attractive woodland and brush.

Eventually, the path swings right across the stream and continues left tracking the right-hand side of the mini-gorge. You soon emerge above houses, where you follow a signpost (A466 0.3 kms) left, down a little track beside a hedge. Soon afterwards, where you emerge onto a narrow paved road, continue directly ahead down a little lane which weaves an intricate way between cottages and garden walls. The path winds down, using stone steps in places, to reach the road used on the outward leg. Turn left and follow the road downhill to take the lane beside the cider press back to the Sloop Inn car park.

St Briavels
The George

5

Only a dry moat lies between the George's patio and beer garden and St Briavels castle – a splendid setting in the heart of this ancient village and sitting 800 ft above the level of the river Wye to the west. The origin of the inn itself is lost in the mists of time – an echo of the past is a late Saxon or Norman stone cross carving, discovered during alterations and now set into a pillar beside the bar. Much altered over the years, the George, with dark furniture, exposed stone walls, impressive fireplaces and dark beams, is an atmospheric but unfussy pub – a cosy place to unwind after a bracing walk.

The choice of beers, too, will warm an ale lover's heart. Regulars are Wye Valley bitter, Marston's Pedigree and Boddingtons and there's also a guest beer such as Wadworths 6X. Cider drinkers may choose from Scrumpy Jack and Dry Blackthorn and other taps include Stella Artois and Grolsch lagers, Caffrey's Irish Ale and Guinness.

The choice of food is an interesting marriage of pub standards

The Castle at St Briavels – now a youth hostel.

and the out-of-the-ordinary. Alongside chilli, lasagne and steak and kidney pie, you have beef stroganoff, grilled tuna steak and seafood Provençal – with cockles, mussels, tiger prawn tails and scallops. Specials include duck breast sauté, liver and bacon casserole and an uncommon option – whole hock of ham glazed with honey and brown sugar. Vegetarians have an unusually good choice; options include avocado and stilton bake, mushroom, leek and hazelnut stroganoff and spinach, mushroom and celery quiche. Children may have half portions or sure-fire winners like sausage and chips. Incidentally a separate dining room (with an impressive wooden fireplace) is a no smoking area. The inn offers accommodation in three rooms.
Telephone: 01594 530228.

How to get there: St Briavels is east of the Wye just off the B4228 about 6 miles south west of Coleford.

Parking: The George has a car park adjacent and there is roadside parking in the village.

Length of the walk: 2½ miles. Map: OS Landranger 162 Gloucester and Forest of Dean; OS Outdoor Leisure 14 Wye Valley and Forest of Dean (inn GR 558046).

A rural ramble through empty countryside in this 'no-man's land' between the river and the Forest with fine views from the higher pastures. There's also a chance to visit St Briavels castle, now surely one of the most exotic youth hostels in the land.

The Walk

With your back to the front of the pub, turn right down High Street and follow it around as it swings left, leaving the castle walls behind you. Stick to the roadside and gradually ascend to a junction with the Chepstow to Coleford road, just after passing the village school.

Turn left down this main road on the pavement, looking out for Hewelsfield Lane on the opposite side. Cross the road and walk up the residential lane, keeping straight on as it becomes less well surfaced. Immediately before a white painted house leave the lane to cross a rustic stile on your right into a field, well indicated by a public footpath signpost.

Turn left and walk along the edge of this large field, with hedge and lane on your left. Cross the stile and continue past the rear of a house on your left to reach and cross another stile. Carry on across further undulating fields and stiles, still with the field boundaries on your left, enjoying the open, pastoral views. Ignore stiles on the left giving access to the lane and watch your footing hereabouts as the ground has been seriously undermined by burrows – there are holes everywhere!

Eventually you approach a line of woodland and a stile next to a metal gate brings you onto a farm track. Carry straight on to immediately take a stile to the right of another gate and walk on down the track to meet a metalled lane near a house.

Turn right up the lane, flanked by low, moss-covered walls to shortly emerge on a road by a cottage and white gate. Turn left here for a short stretch of road walking between hedges with no pavement – care should be taken with children. After about five minutes reach, on the right-hand side of the road, the entrance to Harthill Court Farm. Cross a stile to the right of the entrance drive and walk diagonally left across a field, leaving a fenced bungalow garden to your left. As you approach the top left corner of the field,

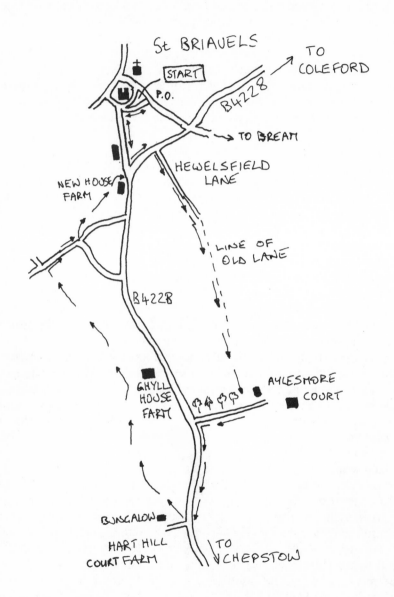

hop over a stile on the left and turn right to pass a gate and go through a gateway on a rough track into another field. A notice here asks walkers to keep off the grass – the healthy sward looks like it's sold as turf. Continue ahead with the hedgerow on your left.

Go over a rise and descend to what was once a junction of gateways but was grubbed up on our last visit. Go straight on into the next field and pause for a moment. Ahead and to your right you'll see Ghyll House Farm beyond the far side of the field. The map indicates a diagonal right route across the middle of the field towards a telegraph pole in the hedge to the left of the farm. If, as we found, the field has been recently ploughed it's a case, literally, of make do and muck. If recently planted and there's no obvious, walked route, you may prefer to avoid damage and follow the right-hand field boundary to the same spot. Here a stile is tucked away near the telegraph pole, almost hidden by an enormous holly tree.

Cross and turn left with the hedge on your left. Go through a gate in the corner of the field and continue straight on through another gateway. In the next field bear half-left across the field to a stile visible in the hedgerow in the far left corner. The unusual circular field beyond may well date back many centuries. Head again for the far left corner to cross a stile by a latch gate – a short stretch of path brings you to a road near a junction.

Turn right and walk up the tarmac road to reach another junction. Pass the road signposted to Chepstow on your right and, just beyond, look to the left for a roadside public footpath signpost and stile. Cross over and walk up the slope of the field, with the boundary on your right. Cross under one line of overhead cables and when you reach a second line, bear left to follow the line of poles to a stile in a gateway to the left of farm buildings.

Beyond the gateway, bear right around the edge of the farm, with playing fields to your left to cross a wooden stile and adjacent stone stile to reach the main road. Turn left down the road, bearing left to walk once again past the school, and follow the road downhill as it swings right to return to the George.

6 The Narth
The Trekkers Inn

There are a number of features which mark out the Trekkers Inn from the run of the mill, but the most unusual is also the most immediately obvious – it's a log cabin!

No long history here then, but the name is in fact a clue to its origins and, it's got nothing to do with walking. The place was set up as a pony trekking centre, developed into a club and obtained a drinks licence, before becoming a proper pub and restaurant only a decade or so ago. Walkers needn't be too disappointed that the pub is not named specifically for them, as they're made very welcome.

The log cabin atmosphere is continued inside with rustic furniture and a dresser in the large, open-plan bar and restaurant area and, like all good cabins there's an open fire – an attractive stone pillar fireplace in the centre of the room. Unexpectedly, you will also find a skittle alley which is used for small functions as well. Outside, the pub boasts an extensive and pretty beer garden sloping down to woodland.

The Trekkers' food has earned it a growing reputation and it's advisable to book well in advance for Sunday lunch, as the place fills up quickly and customers are not rushed through the courses. Throughout the week an imaginative choice of dishes is chalked up, offering starters like melon and sorbet or Parma ham, avocado prawns and home-made soup. Main courses include standards like steaks, but it is the specials that catch the eye; duck breast with orange and honey sauce, Barnsley lamb chops in port sauce, pheasant casserole and halibut in lemon sauce. Vegetarian options might include ratatouille au gratin or mushroom and walnut roast, and there's even a vegan butter-bean casserole available. Children may have half-portion main meals, or choose from the usual chicken nuggets, fish fingers and the like.

A guest real ale such as Marston's Pedigree or Boddingtons Bitter augments the regular beers, namely Freeminer, Felinfoel ordinary and Double Dragon. These appear alongside various keg beers, Guinness and Warsteiner draught lager.

Telephone: 01600 860367.

How to get there: The straggling community of The Narth lies off the beaten track, but is easily found by following signposts east from the B4293 approximately 2 miles north of Trellech. The pub is passed after about 2 miles on a minor road. Trellech is some 7 miles south of Monmouth.

Parking: The Trekkers Inn has a large car park adjacent.

Length of the walk: 2 miles. Map: OS Landranger 162 Gloucester and Forest of Dean (inn GR 526065).

This lovely walk explores beautiful woodland along the valley of a small brook. There are plenty of ups and downs and the walk takes in a viewpoint, as well as an interesting ascent of an old, stone-stepped track.

The Walk

Walk down to the bottom right-hand corner of the beer garden to join a lane which runs alongside it. You face a wooden fence stile to the left of a gate. Hop over and bear right to follow a track behind the gate. Walk down the narrow track with a fence on your left and go through a kissing-gate to reach a broad track. Turn right, then

33

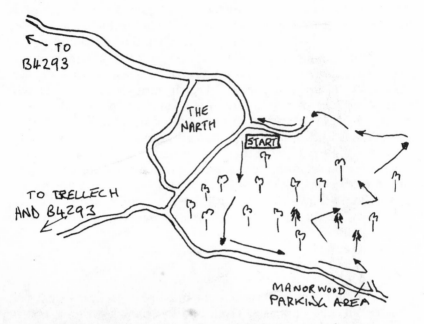

after only a few yards look out for a wooden waymarker post on your right. Immediately beyond this another waymarker post on the left marks a path which you take, dropping downhill quite sharply through the woods. The route is waymarked in the woods using short posts, many of which have lost their yellow arrows, but a white etched band towards the top marks them out. When you meet a broad track go directly across, following a path which crosses culverted Manor Brook. Immediately beyond, bear right at a Y-junction of paths along a narrow and stony path which twists up the wooded hillside.

After a few minutes of steady climbing look out closely on the left for a small path, marked by a poorly positioned waymarker post. If you miss the turn, and reach a road, just retrace your steps for 30-40 yards to locate the path. The path broadens as you pass through a lovely swathe of mixed woodland – trees to look out for include oak, beech, rowan, holly and yew. After a stretch of level, easy walking the path bears left, descending to another waymarker post where you turn left. Go through a wooden horse barrier to emerge into the Forestry Commission's Manor Wood car park. Walk across the car park and take a path to the right of a 'no riding' notice.

Go through another horse barrier and walk on down the clear path, edged with ferns and greenery. The track swings to the left, descending steadily to reach a broad track where you turn right. Manor Brook soon comes into view below on the left and as you approach the stream cross a stile on the left at some wooden fencing. Pass a bench seat and cross the brook by a narrow footbridge. The path climbs left, up some log steps, then after a right turn climbs sharply (but briefly!) to a broad forest road. Turn right here, following a signpost to a viewpoint. You soon reach the viewpoint, now rather obscured by growing conifers, but the bench seat may be tempting. Continue left on the broad track and after about 40 yards look out on the left for wooden fencing a few yards off the track. Turn left here, up a rough, sunken track, climbing fairly steeply between low stone walls. This old track was once an important link with an old paper-making industry below in the valley, which explains the solidly built stone steps.

The path eventually swings sharp left and then right to pass a pretty cottage on your left. Beyond the cottage, ignore a driveway on the right and go ahead on a path between hedges. You soon reach a surfaced road, which continues to climb gently, eventually bearing left into a sort of mini-village square, flanked by houses. Bear right to follow a narrow road beyond Nelson Cottage. After a short while the lane approaches the main road, before which you will find the Trekkers Inn car park on your left.

⑦ Clearwell
The Wyndham Arms

Red sandstone dominates in the attractive village of Clearwell, located on the fringe of the royal forest, and the Wyndham Arms, although much renovated and extended, fits in nicely with its surroundings. Despite being a well recommended and appointed hotel with a restaurant, the large bar manages to retain a pleasantly pubby atmosphere – a trick not easy to pull off. The inn dates back a long way – it may originally have been a 14th-century manor house – and that history is reflected in two unusual 3D hessian tapestries on the wall in the bar. They feature medieval scenes in the village, including the stone cross which stands outside the pub, and certainly catch the eye. Another feature is a tiny bay alcove framed by timber which has just enough space for one table – an attractive little niche. Stone walls, sturdy beams, a huge stone fireplace and darkwood furniture make for a comfortable and relaxing ambience.

The restaurant offers an extensive à la carte menu and table d'hôte options, but walkers are more likely to be interested in the bar menu where there is still a very wide choice. Snacks, served with French bread, include smoked local wild salmon, grilled sardines, deep fried mushrooms and ploughman's platter. Among the main meals seafood platters – hot or cold – stand out, alongside poached local salmon, deep-fried fillet of lemon sole and a selection of steaks and grills. You will find a vegetarian dish of the day and chalked up specials, such as haddock and prawn pie and steak, kidney and vegetable pie. Children have their own menu. At the bar Bass and West Country Pale Ale are the real ales available, alongside Weston's Extra Dry and Blackthorn (sweet) ciders, Murphy's stout, Stella Artois lager and other keg beers.

The Wyndham Arms has 17 bedrooms and offers dinner/B&B packages and weekend discounted breaks.

Telephone: 01594 833666.

How to get there: The Wyndham Arms faces the village square in Clearwell, which is located on the B4231, 3 miles south of Coleford.

Parking: The inn has a large car park adjacent.

Length of the walk: 2½ miles. Map: OS Landranger 162 Gloucester and Forest of Dean (inn GR 572080)

An interesting walk combining attractive pastures and a close look at an amazing pitted and contorted landscape – the result of open iron mining dating back to pre-Roman times. At Puzzle Wood (entry charge) these workings have been landscaped to form an almost surreal walking tour. Elsewhere nature has been left to its own devices.

The Walk
With your back to the pub front, facing the village cross, turn left down the road. Almost immediately, take a little path left (footpath signpost) which leads in a few yards to a spring, perhaps the source which lay behind the village name. It's a pleasant spot with ducks and geese on the narrow stream. Remain on the path which forms a short loop back to the main road, emerging opposite the post office.

Cross the road and take a track to the right of the post office (stile and footpath signpost). Walk up the grassy lane between fencing, cross another stile beside a gate and then turn left to gently climb

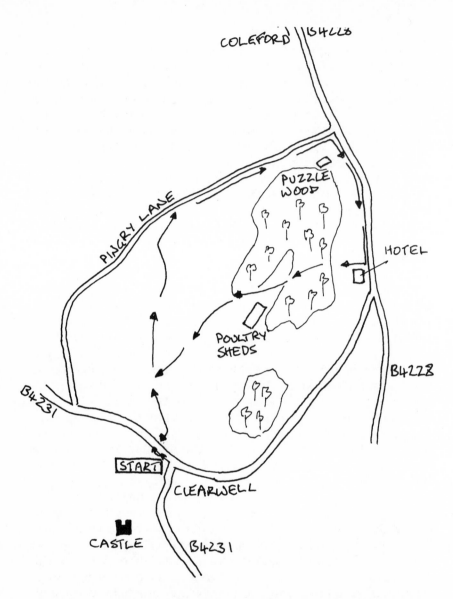

with fencing on your left. Follow the fencing as it bears right up a slope, then as it turns left reach a small bench. Cross a stile on your right and turn left to walk with a field boundary on your left. Continue straight on into the next sheep pasture, ignoring an opening to the left, and proceed along the edge of the next field.

The open, rolling pastures and rural views to the left make a pleasant contrast to forest walking.

Look out for a gate opening by a water trough on the left and go through. Bear diagonally right across the next field, descending towards the bottom right-hand corner. Cross a stile beside a barred enclosure to meet a narrow country lane and turn right. Pass some barns and Pingry Farm on your left and within ten minutes reach a junction with the B4231. Turn right along this occasionally busy road for approximately 300 yards and, as there is no proper pavement, you may feel happier carefully crossing and using the grass verge on the other side. Look out on the right for the entrance to Puzzle Wood which is well worth a visit. Cross the road at this point to use the broad grass verge on the Puzzle Wood side and proceed in the same direction.

After a couple of hundred yards you approach a junction and a wall with a signpost for the Lambsquay Hotel. Turn right down a track beside the sandstone wall to reach a stile opposite a gated drive. Cross and walk ahead towards Lambsquay Woods with the field boundary on your left. Cross a stile to enter the woods and take care to follow the clear path, as the area's bizarre and fascinating terrain is the result of open-cast mining plus mother nature, but old workings lurk in the undergrowth. You soon reach the far edge of the wood and a stile. Cross into a large field and go diagonally left, aiming to the right of a large poultry house complex. Hop over a sort of stile beside a gate and skirt the edge of woods to your right. As you go past the last of the buildings look out for a stile ahead and to the right. Cross this one, and another a short distance ahead to enter an open field.

Bear diagonally left and cross a stile in the left-hand field boundary. In the next field bear right to another stile. There are fine views west to Wales and to your left the walls of Clearwell Castle come into view through hedges and trees.

Head for the bottom left-hand corner of this field to reach the stile you used on the outward journey. Turn left, passing the little bench again, and walk back down with fencing on the right to reach the lane which leads to the village. Turn left at the road to return to the Wyndham Arms.

8 Parkend
The Woodman

A display of disturbingly large saws on the bar wall is in keeping with the pub's name, but forestry has by no means been the dominant industry in this Forest of Dean village. Parkend grew as an industrial centre with furnaces, factories, railway and collieries employing thousands in the area. There's still some industry in or near the village, but green, not industrial grey, is the dominant colour. Engines from the Steam Centre near Lydney puff up to the village on the Dean Forest Railway but this is an exercise in conservation and tourism, not hard graft. The Woodman, built some 250-300 years ago, used to be called the New Inn, and operated as a coaching stop. Now the pub plans to revert to being a real inn, hoping to offer accommodation in three or four rooms.

The Woodman has a cosy, lived-in atmosphere with a large open-plan bar area and separate restaurant. Food is home-cooked with the emphasis on good value and generous portions, but the menu is by no means predictable. Chicken breast with Stilton and cream sauce; roast duck with pork and cherry sauce and salmon and leek pancakes appear alongside staples like steak, grills and beef and ale pie. Specials like venison in creamy sauce and roast pheasant are also worth looking out for. Aubergine and spinach bake, cauliflower cheese and mushroom stroganoff are featured on the menu to tempt vegetarians. Sausages, chicken nuggets and fish fingers are there to keep children happy. Meals are not served on Sunday nights and all day Mondays.

Bass is the regular real ale, supplemented by guest brews, such as Boddingtons, Whitbread Old Dambuster and Fuggles. Strongbow and Bulmers Traditional ciders, Guinness, Stella Artois lager and various keg beers complete the line-up.

Telephone: 01594 563273.

How to get there: The Woodman is situated on the western side of the village of Parkend, beside the Coleford road (marked scenic drive and B4431 on most maps) and about 4 miles south-east of the town.

Parking: The pub has a car park and there is off-road parking in the village.

Length of the walk: 4 miles. Map: OS Landranger 162 Gloucester and Forest of Dean (inn GR 613081).

For the most part this easy but interesting circuit follows one of a number of forest trails which, with cycleways, now lace the area of the Cannop Valley Nature Reserve. Large oaks are the reserve's pride and joy, a haven for wildlife, and a bird reserve section is noted for attracting the pied flycatcher, wood warbler and tree pipit. While the walk sometimes uses now defunct rail and tramways, it also offers the chance to visit a surviving industry – a stoneworks to the south of Cannop Ponds.

The Walk

With your back to the pub front, turn right and right again around the side of the pub. Take a narrow path which runs along the wall on your left to reach a lane behind the pub garden. Turn right along this back lane to just beyond the last house on the right. Here, you meet a waymarked grit cycle track which continues ahead but do not follow it. Instead, turn left along a track which goes into the

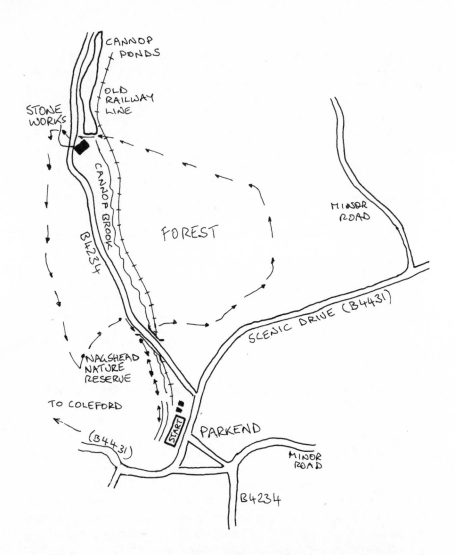

woods between two concrete gateposts. This broad, grassy track swings right and levels out below a lovely stretch of oak and beech woodland on the left, and above a brook on your right.

The track soon reaches a wooden barrier and the B4234 at a bridge over the brook. Cross the road and take a path which leaves the road on the other side, descending right. There is a waymark post with a green arrow here, and these Forestry Commission trail waymarkers are a useful guide for the bulk of the walk. A wooden

The Cannop Ponds.

footbridge takes you over the brook and you soon pass a bridge on the right to meet a cycle track. Turn left along the cycle track then, after a couple of minutes turn right through a horse barrier and join a forest path. The track soon crosses a culvert and then swings left through an attractive swathe of lofty trees. On reaching a stile (do not cross), turn right to follow a broad and rough forest road for a few minutes. Look out on your left for a stile which leads you onto a path through a young plantation.

The track twists a little then meets another wide forest track. Go right for a few paces, then turn left along a gently ascending forest road. The gradient steepens slightly, then as you approach the brow of the hill, take a track on the left. Walk on down the track, soon reach a fence with a gate beside it and go through to reach a junction of paths. Ignore a track on the left and a stile on the right and walk straight on along the forest road with a conifer plantation on the right and deciduous trees on your left. Presently emerge onto a family cycle trail and a junction of paths by a stone-built embankment. Ahead of you is a signpost for the Cannop Valley Trail and other routes. Climb a little path to the left of the sign and bear right to reach the southern edge of Cannop Ponds, a tranquil stretch of water framed by woods. Walk on with the lake on your right, passing a stoneworks on the left – it's well worth pausing a while here, as it is possible to see the stone being cut and sawn.

Immediately beyond the works emerge onto the B-road again. Cross and take a track opposite climbing right away from the road. At a Y-junction of tracks take the left option, along a track which appears to be semi-paved with stone – a relic of industry. Look out for a waymarker near a power line pole to turn left and walk down to a gate and stile. Cross the stile (ignore path to right) and carry straight on along the broad path. This hillside track soon becomes a pleasantly wide and grassy undulating path that generally climbs through open woodland. Cross another stile and continue ahead, passing a rough bench on the right, and ignoring a track to the right marked 'long and short trail'. This area is the Nagshead Nature Reserve, a project involving the Royal Society for the Protection of Birds, as the number of nesting boxes on the trees suggests.

The clear path continues, passing through a latch gate and heading downhill, soon to emerge at another junction of forest roads and tracks. Take the left option, ignore a stile on the right, and walk on down to a gate and enter the nature reserve car park, which has an informative display board. Turn left once inside the car park and cross a stile beside a gate to approach the Information Centre. Continue the line of march beyond the timber building – you have to weave left and right past a fence, ignoring a trail waymarker pointing left. The path heads across the middle of a small field, then re-enters woods and soon descends to reach the road near the bridge you passed on the outward route. Simply turn right on the same side of the road and immediately turn right again past the wooden barrier to rejoin the track walked earlier. The path leads you back to the concrete posts on the outskirts of the village. Turn right to walk the back lane to reach the narrow path beside the pub.

9 Moseley Green
The Rising Sun

Deep in the heart of the forest, the Rising Sun is now a focus for ramblers, cyclists, cavers and trippers – but it wasn't always like this. It was built in the early 1800s to cater for colliers working at the ten pits which, astonishingly, once operated within a ½-mile radius.

With scarcely a trace left of those rumbustious days, the pub now stands isolated in a large clearing well away from main roads and makes good use of the space available. To the rear of the pub a large pond is an attractive feature, and there are tables and chairs scattered about, as well as bench seating on a lower level near a children's play area. Along the front of the pub a large patio with good views is the place to be when the sun shines. Barbecues are laid on during the summer and you might even enjoy brass band entertainment!

The interior is largely open plan, with darkwood chairs and benches in the main bar area, plusher seating in a side room and a pool table at one end. There is a function room and skittle alley downstairs.

All meals are prepared and cooked on the premises and alongside pub standards like steak and kidney pie and shepherd's pie there are more unusual dishes, such as Forest casserole (steak) and cod hot pot. Specials might be lamb, chicken or vegetable balti with naan bread, or broccoli bake. Children have a value-for-money menu with shepherd's pie making a rare appearance among the chicken nuggets and other usual items. Vegetable quiche, lasagne, curry, and cauliflower cheese are typical offerings for non meat-eaters. Meals are not served on Monday evenings. Among the good range of taps at this freehouse are two real ales. Flowers Original is the regular beer, with guest brews like Bunces Old Smokey or Hook Norton Best making an appearance. Gold Label West Country cider is joined by Strongbow and Scrumpy Jack, and you will always find Murphy's stout and Stella Artois lager alongside keg beers and other lagers.

Telephone: 01594 562008.

How to get there: Although positioned well off the beaten track, the Rising Sun is easy to find. Moseley Green is signposted south from the Blakeney to Coleford road (formerly the B4431, now unclassified but signposted as a scenic drive) about 4 miles north-west of Blakeney. Some 400 yards after turning off, you will find the pub on the right, set well back from the road.

Parking: The pub has ample car parking space.

Length of the walk: 2½ miles. Map: OS Landranger 162 Gloucester and Forest of Dean (inn GR 632087).

From degradation to recreation, this walk encapsulates the fascinating story of the Forest of Dean. It is based on the site of an old colliery, New Fancy, whose tip has been transformed from eyesore to tourist viewpoint. Cleaned up and landscaped, former rail and tram lines through the woods have been turned admirably into pleasant paths and cycleways. The start of the circuit at New Fancy is marked by a prominent signpost – it's a forest trail, waymarked with red arrows on posts.

The Walk

With your back to the rear of the pub facing the pond, take a rough

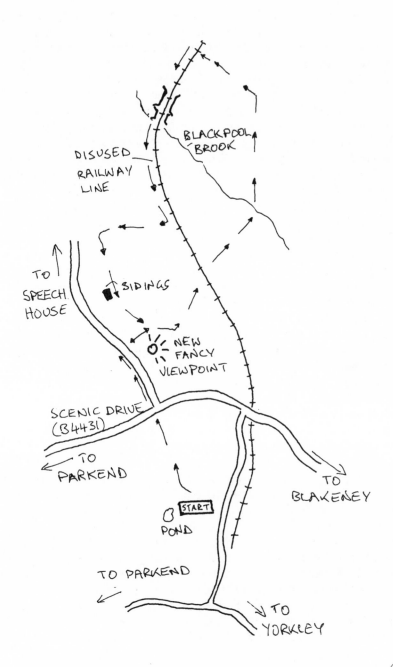

BLACKPOOL BROOK

DISUSED RAILWAY LINE

TO SPEECH HOUSE

SIDINGS

NEW FANCY VIEWPOINT

SCENIC DRIVE (B4431)

TO PARKEND

TO BLAKENEY

START

POND

TO PARKEND

TO YORKLEY

track climbing half-right into the trees from the end of the approach road. You soon reach a broad forest road. Turn right along it, flanked by delightful broadleaved woods. Go around a barrier and continue straight on to emerge beside a road junction. Cross carefully and walk up the road opposite, signposted to Speech House. After 200 yards on the road – there are grass verges – turn right into the New Fancy Viewpoint car park. You can't miss the viewpoint, actually the remnant of a much larger spoil tip, ahead of you. In fact the whole car parking area was once part of the vast tip, now landscaped and planted. The walk continues by swinging left as you enter the car park, leaving the grassed-over tip well to the right. Whether you divert to climb to the top now or at the end of the walk is up to you, but the effort is well worth it for the panoramic view over miles of trees.

The path drops down right from the trail signpost to join a level grit-surfaced track where you turn right along it. You soon reach a broad forest road and turn left – this was once an avenue of lime trees planted in about 1810 and some remain. At a Y-junction, take the right option and cross the cycle track, which follows the course of the Severn and Wye Mineral Loop Line railway built to serve the coal mines in 1872. The last train used the line in 1953. Continue straight on down the tree-lined avenue to reach a four-way junction of paths and turn left. The track swings right, ignoring a green track continuing ahead. Proceed up the track through attractive woodland, which has mature broadleaved trees as well as the ubiquitous conifers. The area around here was apparently used during World War II as an ammunition dump by the US army, so be especially careful with cigarette ends!

At another crossroads, go left and continue up the gently ascending forest road. Just before reaching the crest of the rise go left at a path junction onto a narrower surfaced track. You soon cross a railway bridge which took the loop line over a forest ride below. Continue over a newly built bridge with wooden railings immediately beyond – this crosses the route of a planned railway line which was never completed. After 100 yards or so look out for a pillar on the right of the track with a number 6 – the bit of rusting fence post beside it is in fact a piece of the old railway track.Walk straight on, ignoring a track to another forest road on the right. Continue on the path, parallel with that track above you to the right. You are now actually on the bed of the old loop railway line for a stretch. When you reach a path junction, with the track ahead waymarked as a cycle track, turn right over a small stream (there is another piece of railway line just here). Immediately beyond the streamlet turn left down the forest track, and soon turn right (waymarked) onto a less well surfaced grassy path.

This section, climbing gradually between ranks of conifers, seems to go on a bit, but after a while turn left onto another green track. This soon forks and the left option follows a bumpy bank through trees, avoiding a waterlogged section to the right. This is a pretty part of the walk, crossing little streams by walkways. Presently, bear right to rejoin the good track and turn left. The impressive stone structure which looms up on the right marks the site of Gravitation Shunting Sidings. Cross a stile over a fence and take a level grit path to the left of the wall – the line of an old tramway.

After a short distance you return to the start of the forest trail, where you turn right to climb diagonally back to the car park. From here retrace steps left down the road. Cross at the junction and go ahead back up the forest track. Where it swings right, continue straight ahead past a barrier, to take another forest road. Where it swings right, bear off left for the path back to the Rising Sun.

10 Newland
The Ostrich

Located opposite the churchyard, in the heart of picturesque Newland village, is the Ostrich Inn – as appealing a village pub as you could wish to find. Untouched by the dead hand of corporate pub prettifiers, the pub's two rooms are packed with ancient-looking wood panelling, settles, tables and chairs. Low ceilings, plastered walls and a large open log fire in the larger room (with bar) create a cosy, no-rush-to-leave atmosphere. The inn's exotic name is probably associated with a prominent local family – the Probyns – who used the ostrich as an emblem in the 18th century. The building itself is thought to date back to the late 16th century.

Tradition is determinedly kept up in the choice of beers. There's only one keg pump at the bar – Dortmunder Union lager – but eight handpumps supply a constantly changing range of real beers. There's always one dark beer or stout, such as RCH Old Slug Porter, and the ale choice when we called included Marston's Pedigree, Shepherd Neame Spitfire and Golden Arrow. Weston's Old Rosie is the regular cask cider. Non-beer drinkers may be tempted by one of the two dozen malt whiskies, or by the good wine list, and there is obviously a good choice of bottled drinks.

The menu is unusually varied and original and it's hard to pick just a few examples. Starters may include Stilton and walnut pâté, wild mushroom croque, pigeon with laverbread (seaweed) and devilled mushrooms. For a main meal you could have roast partridge with Madeira sauce, venison medallions in wild mushrooms, steak and oyster pie or lamb and apricot pie. Fish options might include turbot du patron – a fillet in seafood and kummel sauce – and Dover sole stuffed with crab meat. Vegetarians, too, have a varied choice, such as nut balls in wild mushrooms and vegetable balti with naan bread.

One point for families to note is that while children of any age are welcome in the attractive beer garden to the rear, lack of space means that only over-14s are allowed in the pub rooms. It's well worth a visit – just choose a fine day if you are bringing the family! The Ostrich is still a genuine inn, offering accommodation in one double and one twin room.

Telephone: 01594 833260.

How to get there: The Ostrich can't be missed opposite the churchyard in the centre of Newland, which lies on the B4231 between Redbrook and Clearwell and about 2 miles south-west of Coleford as the crow flies.

Parking: The pub has no car park but there is roadside parking in front and elsewhere in the village.

Length of the walk: 3½ miles. Map: OS Landranger 162 Gloucester and Forest of Dean (inn GR 554095).

A lovely circuit of easy walking which explores quiet woodland, a delightful 'hidden' valley and open pasture. It also allows the chance to visit magnificent All Saints church, known as the Cathedral of the Forest, which dates back to the 13th century.

The Walk
At the front of the pub, go through the gate opposite into the churchyard. Follow the surfaced path to the left of the church to a gate in the far left corner of the churchyard – though it's well worth

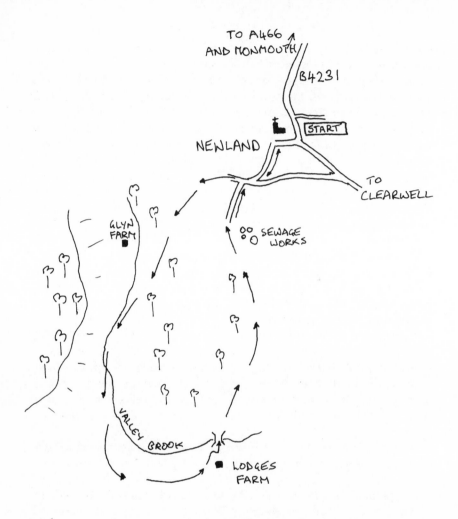

taking some time out to look inside the fine church. At the gate you will see a lane ahead of you and to the left. Follow this lane, descending quite steeply past houses and between walls, to another lane where you turn right. Walk straight on, passing a lane coming in from the left (used on the return leg). The road soon peters out and you continue ahead on what is now a narrow, rocky track climbing between trees and hedges. The track climbs steadily but easily, eventually reaching a junction of paths at a forest road. Cross over and take the path to the left, marked by two sawn-off telegraph poles. Ignore another path leaving the road to the right.

This little path descends steadily to the left through very attractive woodland flanked by ferns and greenery. Soon reach and cross directly over another track, continuing the same line of march on a downhill path. Beyond a stile on the edge of a pasture your route proceeds towards the bottom left corner of the field. The map indicates a straight diagonal route across the slope, but there's now a clear meandering path, probably etched by horses, which reaches the same spot. Here you meet a broad level track and turn left through a gateway. The track follows the bottom of a pretty valley, with pastures topped by woods on both sides. Pass a pool lined with what look like shooting butts on your right, and continue with the stream on your right, going through a series of gates.

Eventually you cross the brook by a little bridge and shortly afterwards, as you come in line with a grand farmhouse above you on the right, leave the track to walk straight ahead to a gate and cross the stile beside it. Carry on in the same direction on the broad grassy track, with the brook below you, now on the left. Views ahead and behind of the peaceful vale are glorious from here, as the track begins to curve left around the head of the valley. The track soon approaches a fine stone farmhouse and goes through a gate. Swing left on the level path to pass below the farmhouse, going through gaps in two wooden fences. Beyond the farmhouse you approach a line of fencing by a bridge over the brook. Hop over a low section of wooden fencing on your right and turn left down the road to cross the bridge and go through a gateway.

Walk on up the rough road which bears right and climbs gradually before levelling out. This well surfaced lane soon enters a quiet valley, surrounded by woodland and generally alive with birds. Follow the lane for about a mile in total back to the village and you can make good progress – we were delayed as we stopped to admire a kestrel perched on a nearby tree and an enormous buzzard patrolling overhead. Eventually you pass a sewage works on the right and join a metalled road. Ignore the right fork which leads to the works site and carry straight on. Soon reach a house and a T-junction with the lane you used earlier. Turn right and then almost immediately left, to climb back up the narrow, steep road to the churchyard and the Ostrich on the far side.

⑪ Upper Soudley
The White Horse Inn

Very much a village local, visitors are nevertheless promised a warm welcome from the regulars – they include, according to the landlord, more than a fair share of characters! Like so many pubs in this area, the White Horse was once associated with industry – in this case the railway. The station once stood next door and the line, now defunct, ran alongside. The pub is bigger than it looks from outside, with a public bar, a roomy, comfortably furnished lounge and a skittle alley which doubles as the venue for occasional entertainment. As you'd expect in a local, you will find there's also a poolroom and darts. An attractive and spacious beer garden with bench seating completes the facilities.

This friendly freehouse offers Everard's Tiger and West Country Pale Ale real ales, plus Stowford Press draught cider, Murphy's stout and, of course, keg beers. Food is traditional pub fare, with the emphasis on generous portions and reasonable prices. Steak, scampi, lasagne and cottage pie are on the menu, along with less predictable offerings such as chicken chasseur and salmon and cod bake. Curry, lasagne and chilli is the choice for vegetarians, while children are catered for with pizza, sausage and burgers.

One point to bear in mind is that daytime opening hours vary, especially in winter. On Fridays and at weekends the pub is sure to be open at lunchtime; during the week it's worth a phone call in advance to be on the safe side. However, the landlord is happy to open up specially for a party wishing to eat and drink!

Telephone: 01594 825968.

How to get there: The White Horse is located in the hamlet of Upper Soudley, on the B4227 about 3 miles south of Cinderford.

Parking: The pub has a large car park adjacent.

Length of the walk: 2 miles. Map: OS Landranger 162 Gloucester and Forest of Dean (inn GR 658105).

This simple, easy circuit around a series of man-made ponds is packed with interest. Created for fish-farming in the last century, the ponds, surrounded by glorious forest, are now a freshwater wildlife haven and a designated Site of Special Scientific Interest. The paths are well made, almost level and should pose few problems for baby buggies or wheelchairs.

The Walk

To avoid a few hundred yards of road walking go through a little gate in the fence at the rear of the pub car park and turn left along a path. Soon join a surfaced lane which drops down to the right. Turn left at a junction and the lane emerges beside the main road. Cross the road carefully and turn right along the pavement. After about 100 yards reach the first of the Soudley Ponds on your left and a choice of gates. You can walk around the pools clockwise or anti-clockwise. I prefer the clockwise circuit, which uses the left-hand (nearest) gate, but either way it's worth spending a few minutes at the displays just inside the other gate a few yards way. These illustrate the waterfowl and wildlife likely to be seen on the walk.

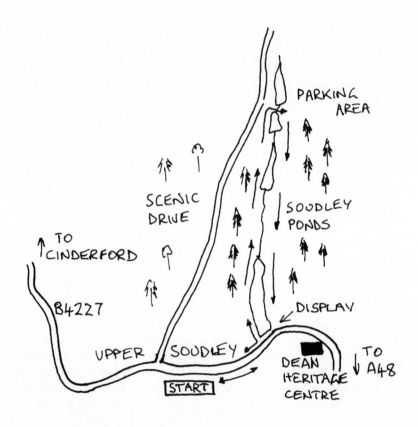

Route directions could hardly be simpler. Assuming a clockwise walk, go through the left gate and walk ahead on the clear, well surfaced path. The first of the lakes is the broadest, and the reed-lined sheet of water, surrounded by awesome fir trees – reaching 140ft tall – is enough to encourage the fastest-paced walker to dawdle and admire. The good track continues beyond the pool, passing an overgrown interlude before reaching the second stretch of water. Ignore a footbridge on the right and continue to the left of the long, narrow pool. There's another scrubby patch before the third pond is reached, with a miniature outfall cascade at its dam.

Carry on around a barrier across the track to reach a metalled road. Swing right to the Blaize Bailey Viewpoint car park, passing another pool to the left which has no obvious path around it. Continue bearing right around the top end of the third pool to start

The Dean Heritage Centre.

the homeward stretch. The track – still well surfaced, level, and even broader than the outward section – goes around another barrier and proceeds all the way beside the pools back to the roadside gate and displays. A left turn at the roadside will take you to the Dean Heritage Centre, the entrance to which can be seen on the other side of the road a short walk away. A visit is highly recommended. A right turn, of course, leads back towards the White Horse.

⑫ Speech House
The Speech House Hotel

A grand building in a grand setting, deep in the heart of the Forest of Dean, the Speech House Hotel has a pedigree few others can match. Built in 1676 as a hunting lodge for Charles II, it was the venue for the Forest administration – the Verderers' court, or Speech court, hence the name. The Verderers' court still meets in the building though now it's a hotel, albeit a tiny one with only fourteen bedrooms. Its central, convenient position makes it a popular port of call and the unusually attractive beer garden in the grounds is a busy place on summer weekends.

Much as you'd expect in an upmarket hotel, the word plush comes to mind when describing the decor. The two small bars on the left side of the building are comfortable, however, and a long way removed from the 'lobby' atmosphere often associated with hotels – though muddy boots are best left outside.

Bass is the regular real ale, occasionally joined by guests such as Ruddles County or Wadworths 6X. Also on offer are Dry Blackthorn cider, Kronenbourg 1664 lager and Beamish stout. The bar menu includes standards like prawn cocktail and soup for starters, but also has some more adventurous options such as baked mussels with herb butter, Madeira marinated herrings and game pâté. Main course options include baked fillet of salmon in pastry, creamed eggs with salmon and chives croissant and home made steak and mushroom pie alongside safe bets like rump steak, lasagne, deep fried plaice, filled jacket potatoes and Cheddar or Stilton ploughman's.

Telephone: 01594 822607.

How to get there: The Speech House is beside the B4226 in the heart of the Forest, about half way between Coleford and Cinderford.

Parking: The hotel has its own car park to the rear and there are free Forestry Commission car parks within a few hundred yards.

Length of the walk: 3 miles. Map: OS Landranger 162 Gloucester and Forest of Dean; OS Outdoor Leisure 14 Wye Valley and Forest of Dean (inn GR 620122).

If you go down to these woods today you really are in for a big surprise. Hidden away amid beautiful mature trees are imaginative works of art which reflect – directly or not according to taste – the history and natural materials of the Forest. The sculpture trail was opened in 1986 and our route takes in a good number of the installations – the full trail is described in a widely available leaflet.

The Walk

With your back to the front of the hotel, turn right and walk along the roadside verge. After a couple of minutes reach, on the left, the entrance to an FC car park (there is also one on the opposite side of the road).

Go through the car park, passing a loo block, to the far end (the far right, facing it from the road). Here you'll see a short waymark post with a painted blue band at the top – the waymark for the sculpture trail, which we'll be following for most of the walk, though not always following the direction of the waymarks!

On the fringe of the car park a short there-and-back diversion to

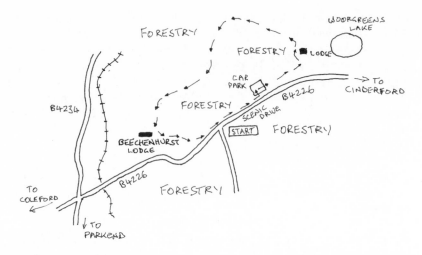

the left leads to the Hanging Fire sculpture – a ring of iron leaf shapes suspended around a tree trunk which looks best in bright sunlight. Our route follows the trail anti-clockwise for a while here, taking the broad track which leaves the car park parallel to the road on the right. This track also sports a yellow waymark arrow: virtually all the many tracks form part of a cycling and walking network which is particularly well developed in this area of the Forest.

After a short distance you will encounter probably the most popular sculpture – Cathedral, a giant sheet of stained glass suspended between the trees. Walking in this direction shows it quite literally in the best light – the treeless background gives a lovely view of the stunning design.

Immediately before the sculpture take a path on the left which emerges on a track by a house. Continue left down through a gate to a track junction. Ignore a stile on the left and go straight ahead on a broad forest track descending between plantations. At a four-way crossroads of tracks continue straight ahead (this time waymarked as a cycleway). Just after a junction with a path coming in from the right, look out on the left for a path, marked with a notice 'Sculpture Trail – rejoin main trail', and follow it.

Shortly, a blue waymark arrow points right for an intriguing view of one of the more striking sculptures (As there is no hunting tomorrow – models of deer in a glade, elusive among the trees).

The path swings left then right to pass nearer the sculpture – a short diversion from the path to the right offers a closer look. Curiosity satisfied, return to the path and carry on. The path goes close by another sculpture – House, a tall steel structure echoing a mineshaft and the industrial past of the Forest.

The waymarked path winds through broadleaved trees, goes directly across an intersecting path and then skirts the right of a pond and swings left to reach the Observatory, a wedge ramp with hidden steps which offer a tree-high view of the Forest.

Continue past the sculpture to reach a junction. The main trail points left, we turn right, following a notice 'Short Cut to Beechenhurst Lodge'. The good track climbs gently to a complex paths junction. Ignore the blue waymark to the left and, counting anti-clockwise, take the second right, a broad path which continues ahead with a yellow waymark and *not* the first right, which almost doubles back.

You soon come to another popular sculpture to the left which although titled Place is also known as the Giant's Chair because that's exactly what it looks like! Built with oak trunks it also conjures up images of Stonehenge. Trying to sit on it is not recommended, but the views from its base across forested valleys are impressive enough.

Continue down the path to the right of the sculpture to reach a path junction. If you wish to visit The Heart of Stone – a beautifully crafted stone sculpture on the site of an old drift mine – continue straight down the sloping track for 100 yards or so and return. We turn left at the junction on a broad track which passes through a gateway to approach Beechenhurst Lodge, which serves refreshments.

Follow the tarmac road to the left of the lodge. It's worth a glance over the left shoulder to see the Giant's Chair framed imposingly on the hillside above. Carry on along the tarmac access road with the lodge on your right and immediately after passing the pay-and-display machine, leave the road for a path on the left, marked with a notice for Speech House and arboretum. Go through a gate and the path, waymarked with red bands on posts, climbs fairly stiffly but easily. Incidentally a fenced-off tree passed en route is not one of the sculptures but a monument to Mr Sanzen-Baker, a former servant of the Forest! Soon reach a gate and the main road. A left turn will bring you back to the hotel in a couple of minutes.

13 Staunton
The White Horse Inn

Regulars and ramblers mingle in this pleasant, unpretentious pub serving the quiet and isolated village of Staunton, which is surrounded by miles of woodland. Although there's a separate restaurant with full à la carte menu, the bar area is very traditional with simple decoration, wooden furniture, whitewashed walls and black timber. The pub has moved with the times, however, as the children's play area in the good beer garden and disabled toilet facilities testify.

The menu, too, is more adventurous than your standard local. The pub prides itself on home-cooked and freshly prepared meals and you may find, chalked up in the bar, a starter such as potted mushrooms in rich smoked cheese and port sauce and main courses like stuffed cabbage leaves with mince, home-made venison pie or fillet steak topped with Stilton and rich port sauce. Fish is a speciality, with the choice determined by availability and what looks good at market. Salmon with asparagus, swordfish and even shark find their way onto the regularly changing board, as well as more commonly served fish like cod and plaice. Children may choose from the usual favourites – fish fingers, sausages and the like – and vegetarian options might include mushroom goulash with rice and vegetables, nut loaf or vegetable lasagne.

At the small bar beer drinkers can choose from Courage Directors, John Smith's Yorkshire bitter and a guest real ale such as Bass or Eldridge Pope Hardy Country bitter. Also on draught are Beamish stout plus Strongbow and Dry Blackthorn ciders and a selection of lagers.

Telephone: 01594 833387.

How to get there: The White Horse can't be missed in Staunton which lies on the A4136 midway between Monmouth and Coleford.

Parking: The pub has a large car park adjacent.

Length of the walk: 2½ miles. OS Landranger sheet 162 Gloucester and Forest of Dean (inn GR 547126).

An attractive woodland circuit, visiting the Suck Stone – an enormous boulder lying in the woods – and Near Hearkening rocks which offer fine views. This is also one of the best areas to see deer.

The Walk
From the front of the pub, turn left and walk up beside the road for about 50 yards to meet a side lane. On the opposite side of the road you'll see a little path (with public footpath signpost) squeezing down the back of a house called High View. The path is also marked with painted yellow arrows which become a useful guide for the first half of the walk. The path is clear, but trousers are recommended as brambles sometimes make their presence felt.

The track descends quite sharply, swings right through the woods and climbs a little, then turns left to briefly become quite broad. Almost immediately look out for a path descending to the left. Deeply rutted in places, this path leads fairly steeply down to a forest road with waymarkers on a distinctive triangular stone at the roadside. Turn right up this broad, well surfaced track with fine views occasionally opening up through the trees on your left. Continue until you reach a dip and where the track starts to rise. Above you on your right, and impossible to miss, is the Suck Stone.

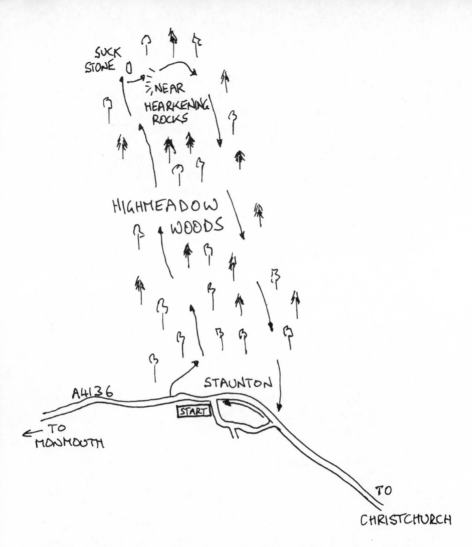

Its enormous bulk looks impressive enough from below but follow the yellow arrows steeply up the bank and, if vegetation allows, walk around the stone – it really is remarkable.

Curiosity satisfied, continue along the path to the right of the stone, clambering up the steep bank through conifers. Boulders and rocks are scattered everywhere and it's the sort of place you expect Merlin the magician to pop up anytime. The path swings right and left and then above you Near Hearkening Rocks loom into sight. The rock has been eroded to form an overhanging shelter – like a frozen surf wave – and the path goes left along and underneath it.

The Suck Stone.

Nature has even provided places to sit! To the left of this sculpture the path climbs to deliver you on top of the rocks. Go right to enjoy the splendid views across the forest to Wales.

Return to where you emerged on top and walk on leaving the viewpoint to the right, following yellow arrows into the woods, soon to reach a forest road. Turn left for a few yards, then turn right onto a path, which shortly swings round to the right and at a junction of three paths in a small clearing take the right branch. This narrow path soon emerges beside a young plantation on your left with good open views – all these trees can become a little oppressive. Continue along this clear path with a forest lodge visible through a coppiced hedge to your right. Not far beyond that go left at a path junction and the route descends a little. At a junction of three paths take the one straight ahead which climbs gradually through coppiced woodland.

Eventually reach a broad, surfaced track and turn right up it. The track emerges onto a side road with houses to the right. Carry straight on through the village, passing Staunton church. Cross the road, proceed along the pavement and the White Horse soon comes into view ahead.

Symond's Yat
The Saracen's Head

The Saracen's Head enjoys the sort of position most pub owners can only dream about. Tucked below one of the most popular viewpoints in the Wye Valley, it's right on the river bank in a picturesque, colourful setting. With plenty of patio seating in front of the pub, it is ideal for alfresco imbibing, and there's usually a lot going on. Pleasure boats dock nearby, flotillas of canoes are often cruising up and down and, perhaps most eye-catching of all, a little man-powered ferry boat criss-crosses between the pub and the opposite bank. The Saracen's Head used to be a stopping place for barges and river traffic and it's good to see the river still busy. Inside, the pub is warmly furnished and welcoming. The bar has flagstone flooring and wooden settles, while the large lounge area is more comfortably fitted out – a good number of seats have delightful river views. Old prints, pictures and stuffed fish complete the traditional ambience.

The building was originally a cider mill, so it's only right that there should be a local real cider at the bar beside a good selection of real ales – Theakston Old Peculier, XB and Best bitter, Morland Old Speckled Hen and Wye Valley Bitter. Guinness and draught Becks lager are also among the pumps.

The wide ranging menu features steak in ale pie, filled giant Yorkshire pudding and minted lamb cutlets, as well as standard pub favourites and a good choice of fish. There's also a daily special such as prawn korma en croute and vegetarians are well catered for, with such dishes as French leek flan, spinach and ricotta cannelloni and broccoli and cream cheese bake. The usual chicken nuggets, fish fingers and so on appear on the children's menu.

The Saracen's Head has nine bedrooms.

Telephone: 01600 890435.

How to get there: Easiest access is via the A40 Ross-on-Wye to Monmouth road. Near Goodrich village take the turning signposted Symond's Yat East. A minor road (signposted) leaves the B4229 to cross the river Wye and leads south to the straggle of homes and pubs on the east bank. The Saracen's Head cannot be missed on the left.

Parking: There is parking near the pub, plus pay and display spaces nearby and a large car park (charge) beside the Wyedean Canoe Centre. The narrow riverside area can get congested, however, and on busy summer weekends it might be preferable to park at the Symond's Yat viewpoint car park (reached via B4432 about 5 miles north of Coleford) and start the walk from there.

Length of the walk: 2 miles. Map: OS Landranger 162 Gloucester and Forest of Dean (inn GR 562159).

A lot of interest is packed into this short circuit – there's peaceful riverside walking, fine woodland and dramatic Yat rock with superb views high above the river, and a chance to see rare peregrine falcons. The climb to Yat Rock is fairly energetic but should present no problems to anyone in reasonable shape.

The Walk

With your back to the front of the pub, turn right down the road and after a few yards bear left beyond the Wyedean Canoe Centre shop to reach a riverbank path, and continue right heading upstream

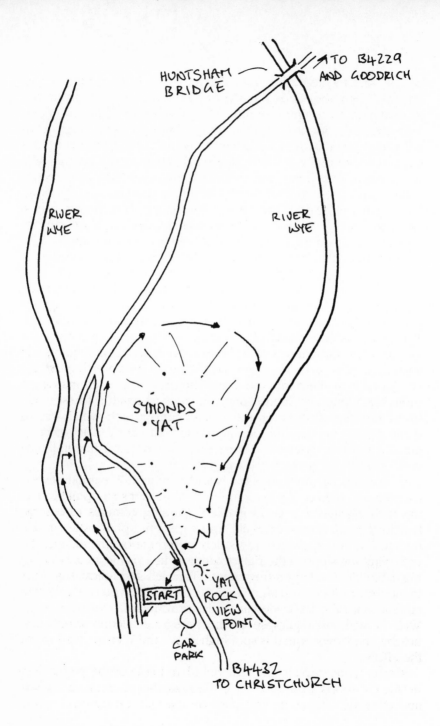

HUNTSHAM BRIDGE

TO B4229 AND GOODRICH

RIVER WYE

RIVER WYE

SYMONDS YAT

YAT ROCK VIEW POINT

START

CAR PARK

B4432 TO CHRISTCHURCH

with a caravan site to the right. The path (waymarked with yellow arrows) continues beside the river, which is often busy with canoes around here, to reach a prominent white signpost marking another ferry crossing, opposite the Old Ferrie Inn on the far bank. Turn sharp right directly across the field to rejoin the narrow road. Turn left and after a few yards leave the road to take a path on the right, waymarked Wye Valley Walk, climbing diagonally into the trees.

Presently reach another road, turn left and after 40 yards or so take a path on the right and continue ascending through the woods. The path soon levels out and then joins a forest track. After a few hundred yards on the track, just as it begins to swing sharply right, take a path on the left waymarked WVW. Turn right when you meet a path near a stile and proceed with a fence on your left. The path descends quite steeply, passes a ruined cottage, and the river soon comes into view below through the trees. Continue via steps to reach the riverbank and bear right at a junction with another path. The path passes in front of a cottage – what an incredibly quiet location – and continues with the river to the left and mighty, ivy-festooned trees to the right. Stay on the broad path which presently swings right to climb into the trees. The path swings left, passing a ruined building, and then climbs via steps to reach a forest track. Cross almost directly over and take a narrow path which climbs quite steeply up the hillside, signposted Yat Rock. The going is initially a little awkward up large rocky steps, but a handrail aids your ascent.

Soon reach a T-junction of paths and turn right. The good news is it's only a ¼ mile to Yat Rock, the bad news is it's all uphill! In fact the path zigzags at a good gradient, passing cottages to emerge beside a road. Cross carefully and turn left uphill. After a few minutes, as you approach a wooden footbridge overhead, take the path climbing steps to the right to emerge in a picnic area, beside a log cabin kiosk selling refreshments. Turn left and follow signposts to the Viewpoint. The path crosses the footbridge you saw earlier to emerge onto the large viewing area, surrounded by a stone wall. With or without a glimpse of the peregrine falcons which nest nearby, the views from this spot high above the Wye are well worth the effort.

Retrace your steps to the rear right-hand side of the picnic area beside the shop cabin, and follow the signpost to Symond's Yat East and riverside. The steps you used on the way up descend to the

The man-powered ferry across the Wye.

roadside. Do not cross, but turn left to follow the path down into the woods. Soon meet and cross a broad track to continue descending a path with reinforced steps. The path swings right to reach a crossing of waymarked paths, where you follow the left option. The clear track continues pleasantly through the trees, descending steadily but not too sharply, and you soon pass the rear of a timber-framed building. Pass the Forest View Hotel on your right and then walk on beside wooden fencing to emerge below the Royal Hotel on the riverside. Turn right along the narrow road with the river on your left to return to the Saracen's Head.

15 Goodrich
Ye Hostelrie

The extraordinary, ornate exterior of Ye Hostelrie might not be quite grand enough for royalty, but there is a link with Buckingham Palace. The pseudo-Gothic stone turrets and pinnacles adorning the pub in this peaceful Herefordshire village were the fancy of 19th-century architect Sir Edward Blore who also had a hand in the Palace and Windsor Castle! While he worked on Goodrich Court, now demolished, he altered the façade of the pub which stood in its grounds. Its towers don't match those of mighty Goodrich Castle nearby, but the inn building, believed to date back as far as 1625, certainly stands out from the crowd. Inside is less fancy, with a modestly sized bar/lounge, plushly but not extravagantly furnished, and a small side room. Black beams and prints on the wall complete the unpretentious decor.

Bar food is equally unfussy. There are standard items like steaks, chicken, gammon and home-made steak and kidney pie, and spicier options such as chicken tikka masala and chilli con carne. Specials may include smoked mackerel salad and hot chicken curry. As well as salads and a good choice of fish dishes, vegetarians are offered provençal vegetable lasagne.

Bass is the real ale on draught, alongside Beamish stout, Stowford Press cider, Caffrey's and Worthington Best Bitter, Carlsberg Export and Carling Black Label lagers. A welcoming feature of the pub is its beer garden, which has a patio area with benches beside a large patch of grass dominated by an enormous apple tree. Children of any age are welcome here, but under-14s are not allowed in the bar.

Ye Hostelrie is a real inn, with eight bedrooms and an evening restaurant.

Telephone: 01600 890241.

How to get there: The village of Goodrich is located east of the A40, 6 miles north of Monmouth. There is a choice of signposted approaches from the A40. Depending on which one is taken, you'll pass Ye Hostelrie either a short distance before or just beyond the turning for Goodrich Castle.

Parking: There is a car park adjacent to the pub and a large free car park serving castle visitors.

Length of the walk: 2½ miles (including excursion to the castle). Map: OS Landranger 162 Gloucester and Forest of Dean (inn GR 575195).

Good views are gained quickly and relatively painlessly on this walk which takes you to a triangulation point and a ruined folly overlooking the Wye and a vast swathe of countryside. It's short enough to allow plenty of time to visit Goodrich Castle – a fine, atmospheric stronghold started in the 12th century. It is owned by English Heritage and there is an entry charge.

The Walk

With your back to the front of the pub, turn left and walk back to the clearly signposted entrance to the car park and picnic area associated with Goodrich Castle. Either visit now – it only takes a few minutes to walk through the car park to reach the castle and ticket kiosk – or wait until you complete your walk. From this point, take the left fork road, signposted Courtfield and Welsh Bicknor.

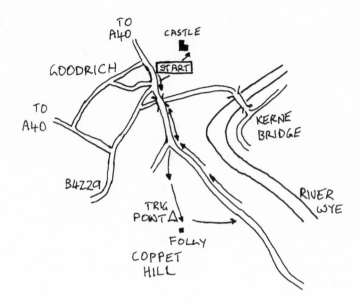

Walk on up the narrow road, flanked by high hedges, and soon cross a bridge high over the road from Kerne Bridge. There are good views here across the Wye to the east.

Shortly after passing a house on the right, reach a fork in the road. Take the right option but after only a few yards up the slope, look left for a footpath signpost marking routes on Coppet Hill Common – there is a small triangular road junction here and the signpost is positioned beside the top road. The route is well waymarked with mauve arrows from here. Walk up into the wood on reinforced steps, climbing fairly steeply as the path snakes up the hillside. Pass a rocky outcrop on the left, then the path soon switches to the other side of the hill, where huge boulders litter the slope. Views open out to the right and shortly afterwards follow signposts left and then immediately right. The path rises gradually across bracken-covered hillside and soon becomes broad and grassy as it approaches a triangulation point pillar. Carry on past the pillar (ignore a path to the left and pass a signpost on the left for the moment) to reach the ruins of a folly, which for the energetic provides a high seat on a wall to admire the broad view.

The triangulation point on Coppett Hill.

Return to the signpost and follow the mauve arrow indicating a path descending through woods. The path soon picks up a stone wall on the right and this is closely followed on a long descent through tangled trees – some even equipped with Tarzan lianas! Eventually the path emerges on top of a steep bank. Don't follow traces of routes dropping steeply over the edge, instead, bear right along the path which soon drops down to a road.

Turn left along this quiet, tree-lined road, passing houses and a telephone box. As the road turns left, keep an eye out on the right for a fine view of Goodrich Castle in the mid-distance. Shortly afterwards reach the Y-junction you met on the outward route. Keep right to cross the bridge again and continue back to the village, passing the turning for the castle again to return to the pub.

16 Howle Hill
The Crown

Hidden away on a hillside in the depths of quiet Herefordshire countryside, the Crown is a fine example of an old local extending its appeal without selling its soul! Dating back to 1857, it once doubled as a bakery for the village – there's still an old oven in the wall of a side room. Locals are now joined by visitors from farther afield, drawn by sweeping views from the attractive beer garden and, more importantly, good beer and food. This well maintained pub is simply but tastefully furnished, without frills, and seating is comfortable on darkwood furniture. At the wood-framed stone bar, this freehouse usually serves West Country Pale Ale and Fullers London Pride, straight from the barrel, and there's also Stowford Press cider, Stella Artois lager, Murphy's and keg bitter and lager.

Food is genuinely home-made using local produce where possible. This includes, implausibly, wild boar! The animals run free in a fenced enclosure close to the walking route and one recipe to make a pig of yourself on is wild boar with juniper berry sausages. Menu options include bresaola as a starter. This speciality

An old cider press, seen near the pub.

of the house is cured beef marinaded in red wine served in very thin slices like Parma ham. Choices alongside steaks on the main course menu include bacon, mushroom and pasta bake; chicken korma; goujons of plaice and fresh wholetail king scampi.

Specials might feature grilled monkfish tail, wild boar sausages or a vegan option – tomato and basil soup with jacket potato and bread. Other vegetarian dishes include macaroni cheese and vegetable curry. Note that meals are not available all day Monday or Tuesday lunchtime.

Accommodation is offered in one room.

Telephone: 01989 764316.

How to get there: The hamlet of Howle Hill is signposted east from the B4228 about 3 miles south of Ross-on-Wye. At the top of the hill follow a sign for Howle church at a crossroads and the pub (signposted) is off the lane to the left, at the bottom of a steep drive.

Parking: The pub has a large car park.

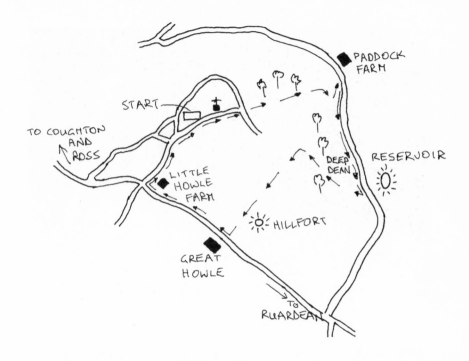

Length of the walk: 2½ miles. Map: OS Landranger 162 Gloucester and Forest of Dean (inn GR 608207).

A rewarding walk through crowd-free woodland and pastures using leafy bridleways and quiet lanes. There's a chance to see wild boar (not running free!), visit an Iron Age hillfort and enjoy some fine views over wooded hillsides.

The Walk

Walk back up the pub entrance drive and turn left down the narrow lane, passing the church and a few houses. The lane swings sharply right, and as it does so, leave the lane for a narrow, sunken path straight ahead marked by a public footpath signpost. This little track, rocky underfoot, descends quite steeply between hedges to emerge onto a broader flatter section. Here keep a close eye to the left where there is a fenced enclosure some 50 yards away – you may be lucky enough to see a boar rooting away, the source of the sausages at the Crown, and massive beasts they are too!

Just beyond this spot the view opens out for a moment over a delightful wooded valley. Soon reach a broad track and cross directly over to continue in the same direction (yellow waymark arrows) down a sunken path, so deep the banks are over head height. The path bears left and you presently emerge onto a narrow road by a house and turn right. The lane climbs steadily, passing a few dwellings, then as you come level with the banks of a small reservoir on the left, turn sharp right from the road at a bridleway signpost and climb up the narrow, steep lane ahead.

Bear right at an indistinct fork of paths, where the trees and shrubs have almost joined overhead to form a green tunnel. The bridleway soon levels off and reaches a hedge bounding an open field. The track descends for a few yards to the right of the hedge and at the base of the little dip look out for a metal gate on your left. Cross a stile beside it and walk directly ahead up the sloping field to cross another stile on the skyline. Continue straight ahead across the middle of this large field to a gap in the hedge line ahead of you. Beyond, continue straight ahead across the next field heading for the right side of a prominent earthwork with trees. As you get closer well preserved ramparts reveal that this is the site of a hillfort. To its right a paved track takes you the short distance to a gateway and the road by Great Howle Farm. Turn right up the road, passing a rather grand home on the left. The road climbs for a while, then levels out affording excellent broad views. At a crossroads turn right, signposted to Howle church (the pub also has a signpost above the hedge) and walk down the lane to reach the pub entrance.

Ross on Wye
The Hope and Anchor

17

Part of this pub, which dates back to the 1700s, used to be an excise yard when the Wye was a trading thoroughfare; nowadays the craft tying up at the pub's mooring are more likely to be canoes and other pleasure craft. It's a fine setting and the large beer garden on the riverbank is a popular draw.

When you have a pub fronting a once-busy river, it's not altogether unexpected to find it has a Boat Bar. What is something of a surprise, though, is to find boats inside the bar! One sleek craft is suspended from the ceiling – it's called the *Wye Widgeon*, appropriate, as unusually tall visitors might have to duck to avoid it! The hull of another forms the base of the bar itself – a case of buying ales over the gunwales. Fortunately there's nothing twee about the Hope and Anchor, as it's a cheery, unpretentious place which enjoys its riverside position and history without going over the top.

Food is varied and plentiful. Main course options on the bar menu include pitta bread filled with salad and garlic chicken, filled potato skins and pub standards like plaice, scampi, chicken Kiev and roast chicken. The regular menu is supplemented by daily specials such as sweet and sour pork, crêpes filled with chicken and mushroom, beef and Guinness pie and pork schnitzel with caper and onion cream sauce. Children may choose from the usuals – fish fingers, chicken nuggets and so on.

A restaurant extension, the Parlour, is more plushly furnished and serves an extended menu in the evenings. Hancock HB and Bass are regular real ales joined by a guest such as Felinfoel Double Dragon, Robinson Best or Morland Old Speckled Hen. As well as keg lager and bitter there's also Guinness, Grolsch lager, Stowford Press cider and Caffrey's Irish Ale.

Telephone: 01989 563003.

How to get there: The Hope and Anchor is beside the Wye on the western side of Ross centre. Leave the A40 at the Wilton roundabout and take the B4260 across Wilton bridge, signposted to Ross town centre. Beyond the bridge take the first left to approach the pub.

Parking: There is a large car park adjacent to the pub.

Length of the walk: 2 miles. Map: OS Landranger 162 Gloucester and Forest of Dean (inn GR 597243).

This easy but enjoyable circuit begins on the fringes of Ross with a short climb to gain an escarpment with fine views, and returns along the banks of the Wye. It's a modified version of a waymarked route which celebrates John Kyrle, known as The Man of Ross, a generous benefactor to the town in his lifetime, 1637-1724. This was, apparently, his favourite walk.

The Walk

With your back to the pub front, walk to the river and turn left along the riverside path for a short while. Just after passing the Riverside restaurant you'll see a signpost beside the path for the John Kyrle walk. Turn left here away from the river across the grass and past the restaurant garden to the pub's approach road. Cross over and pick up a path beside public conveniences which climbs diagonally right up the parkland hillside ahead of you. Soon emerge on a main

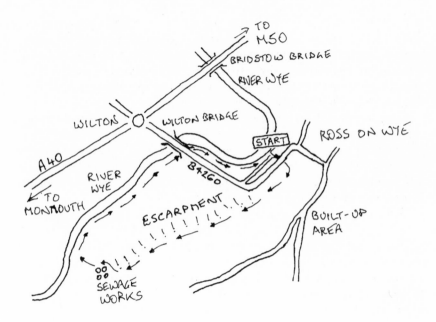

road and turn right for a short distance along the pavement before carefully crossing and picking up a continuation of the diagonal path on the other side below roadside rocky outcrops.

The path soon becomes broader and almost on bedrock before coming to a junction of paths. Take the right-hand path, signposted John Kyrle Walk, and stay on this upper path, ignoring another which descends to the right using steps. Continue on this level escarpment path, with a hedge on your left, through a kissing gate. Now with a field on your left, views open out over scrubby woodland to the river valley below on the right.

As the fieldside path swings left, bear right off it on a path through a kissing gate, waymarked Wye Valley Walk, and soon descend stone steps to the bottom of a deep cut in the escarpment. Go directly across the cut and climb steps out the other side, through another kissing gate to continue along the escarpment, quite pronounced here. There's an orchard and farmhouse on your left, and broad riverside pastures below – as you approach a little dip in the path with a stile beyond, watch out for a nasty concealed step which can catch you out if you're admiring the view and not watching your step!

Go over the stile and carry on beside a large open field, the line of the river becoming clearer through the trees to the right. The path leads through a kissing gate to the right of a filtration works, descending to a junction of rough tracks. Cross a track and bear left, following a public footpath sign, turning the corner of a fenced-off line of conifers. After a few yards turn right at a paths Y-junction (signposted) to walk towards the river on a raised bank with a brook on your left.

At the river turn right to follow the bank path upstream towards Ross. We saw a heron here and were disturbing wildfowl all along the bank – a good excuse for a pause. Stay on the obvious riverside path and as you pass a small island, left behind by a meander, ignore a stile on the right and walk on towards Wilton bridge. Pass under an arch of the fine stone bridge (if this is too dauntingly slippery, walk up right to cross the road and descend the other side), go through a picnic area and carry on beside the river to pass the signpost encountered on the outward leg and to reach the Hope and Anchor beer garden.

18 Carey
The Cottage of Content

A name as evocative as this deserves to have some romantic tale attached – but sadly it cannot oblige. Although the building dates back some 500 years the current name was conjured up only about 35 years ago, but it certainly fits the bill.

Hidden away in a fold amid rolling hills in rural Herefordshire, the pub is beside an appropriately burbling brook and is everything a country pub should be. It's simply but comfortably furnished, with large tables and benches in the large stone-flagged bar, and with pleasing nooks and crannies elsewhere. One tiny niche with space for two small tables was originally outside the pub altogether – the wooden lattice window separating it from the lounge area was once the back window. Drying hops framing the bar and dangling from the ceiling form an attractive rustic touch. When the sun shines though, the benches on the terraced bank behind the pub are likely to tempt you outside.

Tradition is upheld at the bar with a good choice of real ales – Hook Norton Old Hooky and Best alongside Ruddles County and

Best bitters. Weston's Old Rosie scrumpy lines up with Scrumpy Jack and Stowford Press ciders.

The food matches up safe pub standards like home-made pies, steak and deep fried plaice on the regular menu with constantly changing specials chalked up on the board. These might include baked red mullet with saffron and dill butter, roast breast of pheasant with cranberry and kumquat sauce, or char grilled chicken breast with mixed peppers, rosemary and vermouth. When we called a vegetarian option was spinach and mixed nut bake. The Cottage of Content is a real wayside inn, offering accommodation in four rooms

Telephone: 01432 840242.

How to get there: The inn is at the heart of the little hamlet of Carey in a maze of minor roads about 12 miles south-east of Hereford. Easiest approach is probably via Hoarwithy village which is signposted from the A49 Hereford to Ross road. Carey is signposted from Hoarwithy and is about 2 miles to the north-east.

Parking: The inn has a large car park.

Length of the walk: 3 miles. Maps: OS Landranger 149 Hereford, Leominster and surrounding area; Pathfinder 1040 Hereford (South) and area (inn GR 563310).

A simple, undemanding, yet rewarding exploration of this peaceful rural backwater. The walk uses quiet lanes which offer good views and returns along a lovely section of riverside path. If the river is high after rain, parts of this section may be tricky to negotiate without getting your feet wet. It's best left to drier times – a word of enquiry at the pub may save a paddle!

The Walk
With your back to the pub front, walk straight ahead on the road over the brook to pass a telephone box. Carry straight on, following the left-hand option at a road fork, signposted to Hoarwithy and Ross. This quiet road, cutting deeply between tree-lined banks, climbs quite sharply but the effort is short lived and it soon levels out, giving fine views left over the river and meadows – we'll be down beside the river soon!

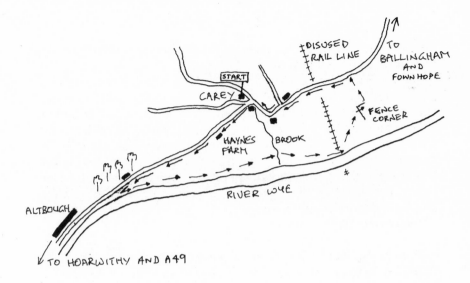

The lane descends steadily and soon approaches closer to river level. Shortly after passing Lower Bibletts cottages on the right you'll come to a large parking area on the left bounded by timber fencing.

Cross the stile to the left of the parking area and walk diagonally right across the field to the riverbank, crossing a shallow ditch which is prone to flooding at high water. Turn left to walk upstream with the river now on your right. The riverside route is easy to follow for a while, allowing plenty of opportunity to admire the quiet scene of meadows and woods on both sides. The path crosses a series of stiles and a footbridge over a brook until, after about a mile, you approach a line of stone support pillars marching resolutely if redundantly across the river – the remnants of a bridge which once carried the Hereford to Ross railway.

Ignore a flight of steps climbing the embankment which once carried the railway line, it's private land. Instead keep to the riverside until just beyond the embankment and pause. Look ahead to the line of the next field boundary – fencing and scattered trees – and trace it left away from the river. You'll see, a fair distance from the river, a pronounced right-hand kink in the fence line. Walk directly across the pasture to that corner and cross a stile a yard or so short of the right turn. Walk on with the fence to your left for a few yards, then turn left to follow the fence line into what is now a tree-lined, sunken track.

85

The remains of the Hereford to Ross railway bridge.

Follow this track, gently climbing, to reach a stile beside a gate which brings you onto a deeply sunken, metalled lane. Turn left and follow the lane which soon passes the line of the old railway and shortly afterwards Rock Farm on your right. Ignore a lane running off to the right beyond the farm buildings and continue ahead. The lane doglegs sharply to the right and descends to the inn.

⑲ Fownhope
The Green Man

This lovely country inn, between Ross and Hereford, has it all. Not only does it look the part, with a black and white timber frame exterior and dark beams inside but it also has tales to tell. One of its former landlords was Tom Spring, the famous bare-knuckle boxing champion who was born in the village. Prisoners were tried here in the 18th and 19th centuries – the judge's bedroom and bars where the defendants were chained can still be seen. Dating back to 1485, the place oozes atmosphere and is deservedly popular with visitors and locals alike.

At the bar there's a good choice of real ales – Marston's Pedigree, Hook Norton, John Smith's Yorkshire Bitter and Courage Directors when we called. Cider drinkers also have a choice – Stowford Press, West Country GL and Strongbow – and Beamish stout can also be found among the taps.

On the food menu there's a range of grills and pub regulars supplemented by specials such as game pie, sweet and sour pork, chicken Kiev and beef, mushroom and ale pie. Vegetarians may

choose from options like vegetable lasagne and mushroom and broccoli mornay and children have the usual fish fingers and burgers. The Green Man carries on the old coaching inn tradition by offering accommodation in nineteen bedrooms.
Telephone: 01432 860243.

How to get there: The Green Man is in the centre of Fownhope beside the B4224, seven miles south-east of Hereford.

Parking: The pub has a large adjacent car park.

Length of the walk: 3 miles. Map: OS Landranger series 149 Hereford, Leominster and surrounding area; OS Pathfinder series 1040 Hereford (South) and area (inn GR 578344).

A tranquil ramble through quiet countryside with the highlight being a pretty stretch beside the Wye, where waterfowl are likely to be your only company.

The Walk
With your back to the front of the pub, turn right and walk the short distance to the village church. Turn right down a side-road just before the churchyard, signposted to Capler. After a short while this quiet back road leaves the outskirts of the village and climbs a rise topped by a prominent building on your right, appropriately named Tump Farm. Keep going on this gently undulating lane, passing dotted homes and farms, with short hedges on the right occasionally opening up pleasant views across the river valley to the right.

After a little over a mile the lane dips to come closer to woodland and the course of the river, still a fair way below on the right. Just before the lane starts to climb quite sharply, look out on the right for a wooden footpath signpost, which leads you from the road onto a track with a private road notice.

A matter of yards along the lane, turn right off it onto a narrow path which descends steeply towards the riverbank – it can be slippery here when wet. At the riverside cross a stile on the right, and walk ahead with the broad Wye slinking past on the left. As you approach a clump of trees on the bank with what look like awkwardly low branches, don't be tempted to stray from the river

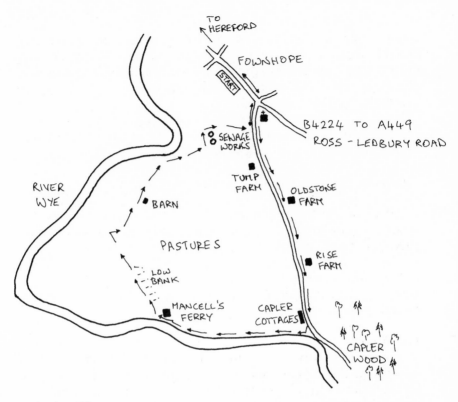

and take the long way around – it isn't easier. Hidden from view is a deep stream channel, crossed by footbridge, below the overhanging boughs near the river's edge. Continue beside the river, crossing two stiles, and as the river begins to turn more sharply to the right, approach a house at Mancell's Ferry.

Don't try to stick close to the river's edge to pass the building as you're likely to end up swimming! Instead look for a stile in the garden boundary a few yards to the right. Bear a little right across the garden to leave it by another stile on the opposite side. Beyond this, note to your left, the jetties which mark this as an old river crossing. Turn right here, away from the river, to walk below a low bank and field edge on the right. Go past a gate opening and carry on to a double stile ahead of you as the bank becomes more pronounced. Go directly across a narrow field to cross another stile (and ditch just beyond) to reach a farm track.

Turn right for a few yards towards a gate but do not go through. Instead turn left just before it (yellow arrow waymark) and continue with hedge and fence on your right. Carry on, with a large tree-studded pasture to your left. As you approach the top right-hand field corner, with gate and hedge ahead, turn right over another gate, with a distinctive, pock-marked tree stump to its right which would be a wood sculptor's dream!

Walk straight ahead, with the field boundary on your right. As the gradient steepens beneath trees and the field boundary swings right, keep an eye out for waymark arrows pointing left across the field towards a tin-roofed barn.

A well-walked path takes you to the left of the barn to two gates. The map suggests a dogleg route here – a turn through the right-hand gate, up the right of the hedge and later a left turn across the field. There is in fact no stile or clear opening in that hedge. The well-walked route on the ground, therefore, irons out that dogleg. After the barn, cross the left-hand gate and another beyond it. Walk directly across a broad field – many boots have made a trail – towards a gate on the skyline and a stile beside it.

Cross the next field diagonally towards the far left-hand corner where a stile is visible in the hedge. At the field corner you'll find yourself above a large house and another stile to its left. Ignore that lower stile – cross the upper stile to the right of the house.

Continue on the left edge of a field and soon approach a small sewage treatment works cunningly screened by conifers. Take a stile on the left and cross the lane beyond to find a narrow path running beside the fenced-off works. After another stile go through a gate on the right to enter extensive playing fields with the village on the far side. Walk diagonally right to the far end of the fields to join the lane you crossed earlier, near a children's play area with climbing frame. Turn left along the track to reach the lane used on the outward leg. Turn left again and follow it around to the left of the church to reach the main road. Here you may wish to step a few yards to the right to find old stocks inconveniently displayed on the roadside at the front of the churchyard. A left turn at the main road brings you back to the Green Man.

Mordiford
The Moon Inn

Until quite recently it was a tight squeeze in the Moon's compact bars. A modest extension has changed that, but not the friendly atmosphere or the charm of this old village pub. Apparently records indicate it was built in 1603 for £17, although other sources suggest an even earlier origin, dating back to the 15th century. The village grew up around a ford over the river Lugg and some form of hostelry is likely to have earned its keep back into the mists of time.

The Moon's slightly crooked walls and roof, with old beams and low ceilings inside, certainly ooze character. The extension has created a larger lounge and restaurant area, decorated in keeping, with a large open fireplace in a wall serving both rooms. Seating in this side of the pub is plusher than in the rustic bar, which serves a regular band of welcoming locals. A beer garden to the rear completes the facilities.

A good choice of dishes feature on the menu, with favourites like grills, lasagne and steak and Guinness pie joining more unusual offerings like chicken Mordiford – breasts of chicken served in cream, leek and cider sauce, steak topped with a wedge of blue cheese, and a medley of seafood which includes king prawns, mussels and langoustines on rice. Chalked-up specials are also well worth checking out. Examples include tenderloin of pork in gooseberry sauce, lamb's kidneys in tomato and garlic, and Italian spicy meatballs. Vegetarians can choose from spinach and cheese cannelloni, vegetable balti and mushroom stroganoff, with the usual nuggets and sausage range for children.

There are usually four real ales on offer with regulars – Bass and Boddingtons – being joined by guest brews, such as Mole's Tap and Morland Old Speckled Hen. Cider is well represented with Strongbow, Stowford Press and Scrumpy Jack and you will also find Guinness among the taps. The Moon does not offer accommodation in rooms, but campers and caravanners are catered for.

Telephone: 01432 870236.

How to get there: The Moon cannot be missed beside a crossroads in the centre of Mordiford, on the B4224 about 5 miles south-east of Hereford.

Parking: The pub has a large car park.

Length of the walk: 4 miles. Map: OS Landranger 149 Hereford and Leominster (inn GR 572374).

The countryside in this area ranks among the most peaceful and unspoilt in the country and this varied circuit makes the most of it. The little brook followed on the outward leg was responsible for a flood disaster in 1811, when a storm led to a mass of water crashing down the valley, drowning a number of people – hard to believe now.

The Walk
With your back to the front of the pub turn left down the road. After a short while reach a waymarker for the Mordiford Loop Walk on your left – do not follow it, that's where you will emerge at the end of the walk. The circuit may be done in either direction, but by walking it anti-clockwise it gives you more time to warm up before tackling Backbury Hill, a modest climb. Proceed along the road to

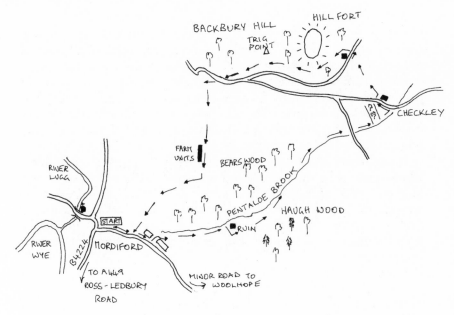

another signpost, situated just beyond a line of houses where the road swings right. Turn left along a path which goes around the rear of gardens to emerge in a small housing estate. The path is clearly waymarked and beyond the third bungalow on the left a narrow track between gardens leads to a stile and an open field.

For a while now the path follows the little vale of Pentaloe Brook, initially with the stream on your left. As you approach a line of fencing, bear right to go through a gateway and meet a surfaced drive, which drops down to rejoin the brook. You soon see a timber and red-brick cottage ruin off to the right. Do not cross a bridge ahead, instead, turn right to walk towards woods, with fencing and the ruin on your left. The somewhat spooky ruin houses nothing more sinister than a horse! Bear left into the woods through a little gate and the path then bears right away from the cottage, passing a concrete footpath sign to Checkley. After a few yards, reach a forest track and turn left.

At a junction of tracks and what looks like a turning place, continue, not on the right-hand track, nor the path turning left over the brook, but straight ahead on the middle option, half-left. A wooden footbridge carries you over the brook and proceed with the stream now on your right. As the broad track swings sharply left, turn right at a waymarker into the woods and over a footbridge.

93

A ruined cottage, seen on the route.

Emerge at the bottom of a large field, with a lovely red-brick and timber-framed farmhouse above you to the left. Walk straight on along the edge of the field, with the brook on your right, cross a stile and traverse another field. As you reach the far end of this field cross a stile in the left-hand corner, located to the left of a corral structure near the brook.

Cross directly over the narrow lane beyond and negotiate the stile opposite. There are a number of waymarked routes here, including the Wye Valley Walk which links with the Mordiford Loop. Do not turn right, following a yellow arrow, instead, go straight ahead with the brook to your right. A couple of stiles take you through a narrow orchard to reach a hedge-lined lane. Ignore a footbridge on the right, and after a few yards on the tractor track emerge onto a tarmac road and turn left. Immediately beyond a group of buildings on your right, follow a footpath waymarker right over a stile beside a gate. Turn immediately left up a sloping field to a stile you can see in a hedgerow above, just to the left of a newly planted and fenced off plantation.

Continue up the slope of the next field, passing by a prominent tree in the middle, towards a bank with a line of trees. An obvious path climbs the little bank, proceed straight up to cross another stile in front of a house and meet a tarred lane. Turn right, then a few yards beyond the house turn left up a track, climbing diagonally into the wooded hillside. This clear track climbs steadily and swings left to traverse Backbury Hill, which is topped by a hill fort. At a Y-junction of paths take the right (upper) route, which continues climbing but soon levels out as a lovely hillside trail with fine views across the valley on the left. Ignore a waymarked path to the right and continue on the clear track, worn down to bedrock, which begins to descend.

At a tarred lane turn right, then cross over and follow a waymarked footpath on the left leaving the lane – do not follow the lane as it twists to the right. Soon reach a signpost with extravagantly long direction fingers and turn left. However, you may wish to carry straight on to visit a picnic site and viewpoint a short distance away at Swardon Quarry and retrace your steps to the signpost. The route crosses a stile into a field, the path heading straight up and over a small rise to a gap in the hedge ahead.

Footpath signs here direct you straight ahead with a fence on your right to a stile. Carry straight on passing tin farm sheds, then a spinney on the right, before turning right – a stile once crossed a boundary here, but it was broken down on our last visit. Go through the gap and immediately turn left. With a fence on your left, walk on down the large field. Note on your left a large oak with a ladder attached – presumably used to access a platform for shooting. Another oak further on has pitons driven in for the same purpose.

Continue with the field boundary to the left and enter woods via another stile. The path descends quite steeply through the trees and you will soon glimpse Mordiford below to the left. Shortly, a fence appears to block your progress, but simply slip off left to drop down some steps and reach a tarred lane. Proceed down the steep lane to reach the road, where a right turn leads quickly back to the Moon Inn.

Other areas covered in the Pub Walks series include:

Bedfordshire
Berkshire
Birmingham & Coventry
Bournemouth & Poole
Bristol & Bath
Buckinghamshire
Cambridgeshire
Cheshire
Chilterns
Cotswolds
Cotswold Way
County Durham
North & West Cumbria
South Cumbria
Dartmoor & South Devon
Derbyshire
Essex
West Essex
Exmoor & North Devon
Gloucestershire
Herefordshire
Hertfordshire
Icknield Way Path
Isle of Wight
Kent – the North Downs
Lancashire

Leicestershire & Rutland
Lincolnshire
North London
Middlesex & West London
Midshires Way
Norfolk
Northamptonshire
Nottinghamshire
Oxfordshire
Shropshire
South Downs
Staffordshire
Suffolk
Surrey
Surrey Hills
Thames Valley
North Wales
South Wales
Warwickshire
Wayfarer's Walk
Wiltshire
Worcestershire
East Yorkshire
North Yorkshire
South Yorkshire
West Yorkshire

A complete catalogue is available from the publisher at
3 Catherine Road, Newbury, Berkshire